A FORGE OF
FREEDOM BOOK

The Thirteen Colonies
~1763~

MILES
0   50   100   200

N
W E
S

Ticonderoga

N. H.

NEW YORK

Albany

Portsmouth
Boston
Plymouth

MASS.

Hartford
CONN.
New Haven

P.
Newport
Providence

PENNSYLVANIA

N. J.

N. Y.

New York City

Trenton
Philadelphia
Wilmington

Burlington

Baltimore
Annapolis

DEL.

MD.
MD.

VIRGINIA

Richmond
Williamsburg
Jamestown

NORTH CAROLINA

Charlotte
New Bern

SOUTH CAROLINA

Wilmington

Charleston

GEORGIA

Savannah

ATLANTIC OCEAN

RIKI

The Maryland Colony

by

F. Van Wyck Mason

CROWELL-COLLIER PRESS
Collier-Macmillan Limited, London

Library of Congress Catalog Card Number: 69–10782
The Macmillan Company
Collier-Macmillan Canada Ltd., Toronto, Ontario
Printed in the United States of America
FIRST PRINTING

PICTURE CREDITS:

Chamber of Commerce of Metropolitan Baltimore, 66–67; Culver Pictures, Inc.,
11, 14, 24, 30, 38, 42–43, 45, 51, 56, 80, 94, 103, 106, 108; Historical Pictures
Service—Chicago, 3, 7, 47, 48, 50, 56, 72, 75, 84, 88–89, 99, 115, 116; From the
Collections of the Maryland Historical Society, viii–ix, 21.

JACKET ILLUSTRATION: The landing of Leonard Calvert.

For my lively young friends
TONY AND PATRICIA BECKER

CONTENTS

a.

*a. First Lord George Calvert (Died
   before ruling Maryland)*
*b. Second Lord Cecil Calvert
   (Ruled Maryland 1632–1675)*
*c. Third Lord Charles (1) Calvert
   (Ruled Maryland 1675–1715)*

b.

c.

d.

*d. Fourth Lord Benedict Leonard
    Calvert (Ruled Maryland 1715)*
*e. Fifth Lord Charles (2) Calvert
    (Ruled Maryland 1715–1751)*
*f. Sixth Lord Frederick Calvert
    (Ruled Maryland 1751–1771)*

e.

f.

PART ONE

LAND OF THE LURKING SAVAGE

1 « FIRST VISITORS

The beautiful little state now known as Maryland lies for its greatest part along both sides of the Chesapeake, the greatest bay within the continental United States. Into it flow almost countless tawny rivers and streams of all sizes.

In early times this low-lying and very fertile Tidewater Country—as this region came to be called—fairly swarmed with all sorts of game. There were countless bronze-tinted turkeys, handsome passenger pigeons, doves, grouse, deer, bear, elk and even an Eastern bison which the settlers called woods buffaloes.

Less pleasant to have around were wolves, panthers (some times called cougars), lynx, bobcats and foxes. Of these the most dreaded by settlers were the wolves which often travelled in great packs and feared nothing.

Waterfowl such as swans, geese, brants, coots and ducks were so many that when flocks took wing their flight darkened the sun.

For the most part soil in the Bay country was very rich, having once been silt on the bottom of an ancient sea that had disappeared. In many places the ground was so fertile that three crops could be grown on it in a single year.

Many different tribes of Indians inhabited the Tidewater Country. For the most part these peoples, such as the Poto-macs, Wicomocos, Pocomokes and Assateagues, were easy-

An early depiction of Powhatan, ruler of many Virginia Indian tribes when the first white settlers arrived.

going and unwarlike because the climate wasn't as harsh as that of New England, and food was easy to come by. Most important of all, most Tidewater Indians lived at a safe distance from the pitiless Iroquois and Algonquin tribes that roamed to the north and west. The great width of Chesapeake Bay also saved them from attacks by the fierce and warlike followers of Powhatan, the great Indian emperor who, in the early seventeenth century, ruled over a great many tribes living in Virginia. All of these Indian tribes have disappeared but are remembered because the rivers they lived upon are named for them.

The Indians of lower Chesapeake Bay were mostly simple, gentle farmers and fishermen. They lived in constant fear of raids by the tall and fiercely painted Susquehannocks who lived near the head of the Bay. The Susquehannocks, althought they were an Iroquois people, were always at war with their kinsmen, the dreaded Mohawks and Senecas. Whooping and howling and brandishing knives and tomahawks, they always attacked without warning and generally at dawn.

One day in the spring of 1524, an Indian youth belonging to the Assateague tribe was hunting along the shore of Chincoteague Island which lies not far off the Atlantic side of a very long and low peninsula now known as the Eastern Shore of Maryland. On reaching a small, deep-water cove the hunter was thunderstruck to see floating peacefully a huge, strange-looking canoe. It was unlike any other waterborne craft he had ever beheld—or even heard of, for that matter. Trees seemed to be growing out of it with great pieces of white or brown cloth hanging from their leafless branches.

The young Indian was still gaping at this great and wonderful craft when suddenly there appeared a party of strange-looking men who wore heavy beards and whose skin was pink-brown in color. Some wore metal hats and shirts that flashed dully in the warm sunlight. In addition to swords and knives, the strangers carried queer-looking, long iron sticks ending in a length of wood. They were covered from head to foot with cloth and leather while the savage was wearing only a necklace of mussel shells. These were the very first white men the young Indian or any of his tribe, the Assateagues, had ever seen.

The strangers had ventured ashore from a ship named the *Dauphine*. She was commanded by an Italian named Giovanni de Verrazano. Because he had been hired by the King of France to explore this coast, it is not surprising that his crew were mostly French.

The white men looked curiously on this bronzed, good-looking and well-muscled savage who wore long and glossy blue-black hair twisted into a tight knot behind his head and secured by a skewer of bone. For a long moment they just stared. Finally, the naked red-brown figure uncertainly raised a hand towards the sky and stepped forward. Although he was badly frightened he tried to smile. One of the Frenchmen, probably intending only to scare the Indian, fired his musket into the air. Terrified by a thunderous report and clouds of rotten-smelling smoke, the youth fell onto his knees. According to an old account: "Worshipping like a monk he lifted his fingers toward the sky and pointing to the ship, he appeared to bless us."

Then a swift and powerful bound carried the young Assateague into a green tangle of underbrush. Instantly he became lost to sight. Fearing the fugitive might have run to raise an alarm, the men from Verrazano's ship cautiously made their way inland over a flat countryside. They found small clearings among towering trees in which sprouts of corn, peas, beans and squash were thrusting above the sandy black soil.

The Indian the French sailor had terrified with his heedless shot belonged, like most of the inhabitants of Lower

Chesapeake Bay, to a tribe of gentle, peace-loving people. They lived by farming, trapping and hunting. The local savages fished from heavy and awkward log canoes which they laboriously hollowed out by fire and then scraped with oyster shells. Indians in that part of the country usually went stark naked save for bone ornaments and feather head-dresses. Grown women, however, sometimes wore short kilts made of soft, gray-white Spanish moss. It no longer grows anywhere in Maryland.

Around 1585 an English sea captain named John Wyth—or White—entered the Bay and made a crude map of its lower parts, but that is all that is known about him. Shortly afterwards a Captain Lane definitely entered the Chesapeake but nothing is known of where he went or what he saw.

The results of that shot fired so thoughtlessly by Verrazano's sailor were not to be felt for almost one hundred years when, in 1603, a ship appeared in Chesapeake Bay searching for possible survivors of Sir Walter Raleigh's Lost Colony. Established on Roanoke Island off North Carolina in 1580, this settlement had disappeared without a trace.

This ship, a small bark named the *Elizabeth*, was commanded by Captain Bartholomew Gilbert. Bad weather drove him up the Bay as far as what is still called Smith's Island. This was named for the famous Captain John Smith, another early visitor of whom we will soon hear a good deal.

Since Captain Verrazano's visit, accounts of that fateful musket shot had travelled far and wide. Its effect had become so wildly exaggerated that when Captain Gilbert with three seamen ventured ashore in search of fresh water, Indians, fearful of this strange power, ambushed the little party. They killed Captain Gilbert and one of his sailors. The other two seamen managed to escape to their ship. Its crew hurriedly raised anchor and returned to England without searching any farther for Raleigh's lost colonists.

It can be seen that by now the simple Indians of the lower Bay associated big trouble with "great sailing canoes" and white men carrying firearms. Perhaps it was just as well that when Captain John Smith, in June, 1608, set out from Kecoughtan (Hampton, Virginia), he sailed in a small, undecked barge carrying a single small sail and was accompanied by only fourteen companions.

This Captain John Smith was also a famous adventurer. He had fought the Turks and killed champions of theirs in single combat. He was captured by them but escaped. Captain Smith figures importantly later on in the early history of another English colony—Massachusetts. It is fortunate for us that Captain Smith was given to writing in detail about his travels and adventures. He also drew maps which, like his journals, were remarkably accurate for that day. Therefore it is easy to follow Captain Smith's route on the two voyages he made to explore all of Chesapeake Bay. He was very brave to do this because he and his followers had

John Smith's voyages led to the establishment of Maryland.

no idea of what terrible dangers this vast and unknown wilderness might hold.

Although Captain Smith couldn't know it, his voyages led to the establishment of the Colony of Maryland. This became the third of the original Thirteen Colonies to be permanently settled. Only Jamestown in Virginia (1607) and Plymouth in Massachusetts (1620) were founded earlier.

On his first exploration of Chesapeake Bay, Captain Smith sailed from Hampton, Virginia, to Cape Charles, which forms the southern tip of the Eastern Shore of Maryland and Virginia. Nowadays it is called the Delmarva Peninsula. His tiny expedition had been so hastily assembled that it was badly supplied. Soon the adventurers were hungry and thirsty. When they went ashore to find water they were met by "two grimme, stout salvages [savages] armed with poles tipped with bone heads." Nobody knew how many more Indian warriors might be lurking nearby in the dense woods.

At first the Indians acted unfriendly, but on seeing how few the white men were and that they were sailing in a small vessel, they welcomed these bearded men in bright breastplates and helmets and took them to meet their werowance (chief) at a place called Accomac.

This chief was a brother to Debedeavon who had been nicknamed "The Laughing King of Accomac." This was probably because he and his tribe were never threatened by fierce enemies, and their land was good and the fish and game so plentiful they didn't have to work hard or suffer from starvation. Until his death Debedeavon remained on excellent terms with the English.

While Captain Smith was serving The Virginia Company at Jamestown in some very important positions, he learned to speak the language of Powhatan's people. The Emperor Powhatan was a hard, shrewd and capable chieftain who ruled over many tribes in Virginia and some in what later became Maryland. As the "Laughing King" nominally was a subject of Powhatan, Captain Smith found it easy to converse with his new friends.

After taking aboard a fresh supply of food and water the white men sailed north until they again ran short of drinking water. They turned into the mouth of a wide river with lush, low-lying banks where great trees stretched their branches far out over the water. Captain Smith misnamed this river on his map by calling it Wighcócomoco. It was known to the Indians as the Pocomoke.

The local Indians at first acted hostile but, as often happened, they soon changed their minds and made the bushy-bearded and badly sunburned explorers welcome "with songs, dances and much mirth."

Smith's barge continued to sail northward over the vast and lonely expanses of the Bay until, near the entrance to the Pocomoke River, the explorers discovered a group of low, well-forested and lovely little islands. They named these the Smith Islands after their leader. They are still called by that name.

Continuing up the eastern shore of the Chesapeake they soon came upon the wide, slow-flowing and very winding Nanticoke River. This is another of the many important streams which flow into the Bay. In his journal Captain Smith wrote:

> By this river dwell the Soraphanigh, Nause, Arsek and Nantiquake, who ran as amazed in troops from place to place, divers got in the tops of trees. Not sparing of their arrows, nor of the greatest passion they could express of their anger. Long they shot, we riding at anchor out of range.
>
> Next day they came (to the shore) unarmed, everyone with a basket, and danced in a ring to draw us ashore. Seeing there was nothing in this but villainy, we discharged a volley of muskets charged with ball. They all tumbled to

the ground, some creeping one way, some another into a
thicket of reeds. There they lay in ambush.

Towards evening we weighed and approaching the
shore, discharged five or six shots among the reeds. We
landed where they laid and found many baskets and much
blood, but not a salvage. Seeing smoke across the river,
we rowed over and found two or three little houses, in
each a fire. We left pieces of copper, beads, bells and looking glasses and returned to the barge.

Next morning four salvages came in from the Bay in a
canoe, not knowing what had happened. We used them
with such courtesie they bade us stay (while they went on
to the village). They came back with about twenty more
and after a little conference, two or three thousand men,
women and children came about us everyone presenting
us with something which even a little bead would so well
repay, that they began to dispute who would fetch us
water, stay with us for hostage, and give us the best
content.

After leaving the Nanticoke, Captain Smith's barge raised
its patched and faded sail and headed for the opposite or
western side of the Chesapeake. At this point the Bay is so
wide that the far shore can hardly be seen. The explorers
found the Western Shore to be a pleasant, well-watered land
with low hills and many fertile valleys. Nowhere did they
meet any Indians but reported the woods to be "extreme
thick, full of wolves, bears, deere and other wild beasts."

For nearly two weeks Captain Smith followed the shore-
line northwards. He was screamed at by fish hawks and
jeered by gulls and terns but the land appeared a vast wilderness empty of human beings.

Now the weather turned stormy and Captain Smith's
companions began to complain bitterly. After so many days
of hard rowing and eating only moldy bread they had become sick, worn-out and discouraged. Also, they had grown

Indians from villages like this were friendly to Smith and his party.

very fearful of this vast and unknown country. They feared sudden attack from lurking savages. They knew that if they were taken prisoner they would die under hideous tortures. After a violent argument, Captain John Smith, though tough and courageous, agreed most unwillingly to turn back.

While returning to their base at Hampton, Virginia, Captain Smith and his men took time to explore the entrance to the Potomac River where for some reason they decided to pan for gold—unsuccessfully, alas. While doing this the white men always remained alert because they knew they were now in the country of the powerful and treacherous Emperor Powhatan.

Once again the explorers ran out of food. Great schools of fishes swam all about so the men tried to catch some. Since they had with them neither hooks nor nets they had no luck. They anchored in a shallow place and tried to take fish with a frying pan! But, as Captain Smith wrote, "We found it a bad instrument to catch fish with." The ever-resourceful Captain and others then tried using their swords for spears and were more successful. Soon they had all the fish they could eat.

It was while fishing in this manner that Captain Smith came very near to losing his life. He was struck in the arm by the barb on the tail of a poisonous sting-ray and was very glad to return to Hampton safe and sound.

Before going up to Jamestown to make a report, Smith decorated his barge with all kinds of bright flags and banners. He was always a considerable showman. The authorities listened eagerly to the story of his adventures up the Bay which probably lost nothing in the telling. Captain Smith aroused so much interest that in less than a month's time he sailed on a second expedition. Among other things he was determined this time to discover the Northwest Passage. This was supposed to be a short route to the Pacific Ocean which would make it quick and easy for Englishmen to reach Cathay (China) and to open up trade with the fabulous, golden cities of the Orient.

On this voyage Captain John Smith sailed up the Western Shore of the Bay all the way to its head. There he found that four great rivers emptied into it close together. Here the gaunt and travel-worn Englishmen met for the first time the fierce Iroquois Indians who were spreading terror, death and destruction through much of what is now New York and New England. The Iroquois also were known as the Five Nations (later they would number six). These particular warriors were Massawomekes, an Iroquois sub-tribe. There were six canoes full of big, brilliantly painted and heavily armed braves.

This encounter could hardly have taken place at a time less favorable to Captain Smith and his men for sickness recently had struck the little group so hard that only five men were able to get about. If the Iroquois found this out, Captain Smith knew the English would be massacred at once. So he concealed his sick companions under a tarpaulin, stuck their hats on sticks, and then in a threatening manner poked over the barge's rail the barrels of wheel-lock and firelock muskets they were too feeble to fire. The trick worked and the Massawomekes hurriedly paddled away.

Because Captain Smith took care to keep his craft under sail, these very tall and powerfully built savages were greatly impressed. Never having seen sails before, they couldn't understand what made the white men keep on moving when no one was rowing or paddling. Captain Smith sailed right up to the Iroquois camp and boldly anchored close inshore.

After a while two fearsomely painted and half-naked Massawomekes paddled out with a few red-tipped eagle feathers nodding in their sleek, blue-black hair. They held up empty hands to show that they came in peace and were carrying no weapons. Captain Smith gravely presented the two savages with shiny little brass bells.

Although neither party spoke a common language the peace sign was made. Soon the rest of the Iroquois, powerful men with lean, scarred bodies paddled warily out to the barge. Plenty of dried peas and squash, bear meat and jerked venison was passed over the gunwales. Deadly spears, bows and arrows and many beautiful, glossy furs were exchanged for small mirrors, glittering blue or red glass beads, lengths of bright ribbon and other trinkets.

To their uneasy astonishment, the Englishmen noticed that the fingernails of these Iroquois had been allowed to grow long and had been sharpened like the claws of wild beasts. With these they could rend and mutilate an enemy at close quarters.

The explorers soon realized that these Massawomekes

The fierce Iroquois often traded with tribes that roamed as far north as Canada.

were the first Indians they had met on Chesapeake Bay who owned hatchets, knives, pots and other articles made of iron or other metals.

Later, they found an explanation: the Iroquois often traded with tribes who roamed even farther north than they did. The metal objects had come from Canadian Indians who had got them from French traders who were called *coureurs de bois*.

This meeting ended in friendly fashion, but the Iroquois vanished next day although they had agreed to trade some more.

The explorers now started down the long, flat and river-laced Eastern Shore. Near the mouth of the Sassafras River they came upon the Tockwoghs. This was a large tribe which had fought recently with the very same Massawomeke war party with which Captain Smith had traded.

Indians appeared by the hundreds and stared from blank black eyes at these bearded strangers. Since the Tockwoghs spoke the language of Powhatan's people, a friendly meeting soon took place.

Captain John Smith was clever. With many loud boasts he told his hosts that the Iroquois weapons and metal articles they saw had been taken from the dreaded Massawomekes only after a hard fight. The Tockwoghs were impressed. They decided the English with their firearms and bits and pieces of armor must indeed be mighty warriors to have overcome the dreaded Iroquois.

The ragged and hungry palefaces then were conducted to a fortified town lying a short distance up river. Here they were entertained with much feasting, yowling song and endless prancing dances. After the entertainment was over, the Indians' werowance gave the handful of guests a generous supply of food and drinking water.

The next tribe Captain John Smith's expedition met were the proud, bright-painted and warlike Susquehannocks. They also were supposed to be man-eaters. The gallant Captain describes them thus:

> Such great and well-proportioned men as are seldome seen, for they seemed like Giants to the English, yea, and to their neighbors, yet seemed of an honest and simple disposition. . . . the strangest people of all both in language and attire. . . . The calf of the chiefest of the Werowances was three-quarters of a yard around and the rest of his limbs in proportion. The goodliest man that ever we beheld.

After that, Captain Smith turned back to Virginia following the Eastern Shore. He hurried because word had come that the Emperor Powhatan was getting ready to make war.

The well-travelled sailing barge barely escaped being sunk in a furious storm (today it would be called a hurricane) but reached Jamestown safely in early September, 1608.

2 « FIRST SETTLERS

To the west and south of the great Bay explored by Captain Smith lay the only English colony in America other than Massachusetts. This was the Royal Colony of Virginia. It was governed by the Virginia Company which operated under a Charter granted by Elizabeth I, the Virgin Queen. The colony had been named Virginia in her honor. The territory granted to the Virginia Company had been only very loosely described. At that time there were no surveyors to measure out and accurately define the Colony's boundaries.

It was understandable therefore that any Englishman operating out of Jamestown could lay claim to any nearby choice piece of territory simply by saying it belongs to Virginia.

Records indicate that the very first Englishman to settle permanently on the Eastern Shore was one Thomas Savage. In 1619 Savage found a place he liked on the lower Eastern Shore, so he brought over his family and invited some friends to come along and buy land from the Indians and build homes there.

Because settlers in Jamestown were suffering greatly from disease, hunger and continual attacks by the treacherous Emperor Powhatan's merciless subjects, it was natural that several families quickly came to Tom Savage's little foothold on the Accomac River.

Surrounded by friendly, lazy Indians, enjoying a mild climate, and with plenty of fish and game to be had without much effort, the new settlement prospered. Before long Savage and his friends were strong and numerous enough to justify sending one of their number to represent them in the Virginia House of Burgesses. This remained the first and only lasting settlement in Maryland for almost twenty years.

The next permanent settler was Captain William Claiborne. A prominent Virginian, he collected some followers and sailed far up the Bay. He landed upon a large, wooded and very fertile island, which he named Kent Island. A man of strong character and great ambition, William Claiborne at once set up a truck house (trading post) which did so well that his settlement grew rapidly and prospered.

The truck house was established under a license granted by King Charles I of England, which permitted Claiborne and his people to trade and make discoveries "in all other parts of North America that are not already chartered."

William Claiborne was one of the most forceful characters in the early history of Maryland. Tall and handsome, he was also shrewd and very determined to have his way. Although a hard and experienced fighter he nevertheless was generous to his enemies when he found them at his mercy.

Sailing from England in a ship named the *Africa* he brought to Kent Island twenty colonists and a plentiful supply of trade goods. On the way he stopped at Hampton, Virginia, where he recruited over a hundred people who were eager to quit the dangers and unhealthy climate of Jamestown. Claiborne's ship finally arrived at Kent Island in July of 1631 and was welcomed by his traders already there.

As soon as he reached his grant, Captain Claiborne bought land from the Indians for a fair price. Soon the hard-working Kent Islanders were making fine crops and doing a flourishing trade in beaver and other furs brought to them by tribes roaming up the Bay and all the way to Canada.

The Kent Islanders' future appeared to be secure and promising but, as events turned out, this was not to be the case. Their rights to the island and their allegiance to the Virginia Company were about to be disputed by George Calvert, the first Lord Baltimore. King Charles I had granted him a charter whose borders surrounded the territory claimed by William Claiborne. These conflicting claims became the source of serious trouble over the next twenty years. They led to warfare and bloodshed and the first naval battle ever to be fought between English-speaking people in what is now the United States.

3 « THE LAND OF SANCTUARY

When news of Captain John Smith's explorations reached England, the first Lord Baltimore, whose family name was Calvert, immediately became interested. He already had visited America and could foresee great opportunities there for freedom-loving people. He had been to points as far apart as Newfoundland, where he founded a colony called Avalon (which failed), and to Jamestown.

In 1629 he left his wife and children in Virginia for a short while in order to return to England and petition King Charles I for a huge grant of territory around Chesapeake Bay and beyond it to the north and west.

George Calvert was a favorite of the King and got all he asked for. In 1631 King Charles authorized a very liberal and most unusual charter. It named George Lord Baltimore and his heirs "Lords Proprietor of Maryland," the only ones with all such broad powers ever to exist in English America.

George Calvert was not the typical Royal Governor sent out to govern a colony in the King's name. His holding was self-governing and an almost independent principality (palatinate). His tenants swore loyalty to the Lord Proprietor, not to the King of England. A Lord Proprietor had very wide and unusual powers. He could appoint judges, pardon criminals, issue money, raise troops and wage war on his own. He could also grant title to land and, if he wished, create a local nobility—something he never attempted.

The charter's most important provision was that the Lords Proprietor were free to give refuge and equal rights to Christians of *all religious groups*—a privilege never before granted. Nor was there to be an official religion in Maryland like the Church of England at home.

This was most important to Lord Baltimore because he recently had become a Roman Catholic. In England Catholics for a long time had been savagely persecuted in many ways.

Therefore it was natural that Lord Baltimore's new colony should become known as the Land of Sanctuary. Almost from the very beginning, people of many beliefs went there in search of religious freedom, for equal opportunities and security under the law. Among these were Quakers, Methodists, Baptists, Wesleyans, Puritans and even a few Jews.

Other important provisions were that, in return for this generous Charter, the Lord Proprietor promised to send to the King at Windsor Castle a yearly tribute of two Indian arrows and one-fifth of any gold and silver to be found in Maryland. Neither of these metals was ever discovered in worthwhile amounts.

Marylanders would not have to pay taxes to the Crown and they could govern themselves locally through representatives freely elected by them. George Calvert got a wonderful bargain for himself and the cause of freedom.

The new colony was named by King Charles I for his Queen, Henrietta Marie, so the grant at first was termed Mary's Land, or *Terra Mariae* in Latin.

Unfortunately the first Lord Proprietor died just before his Charter was signed and stamped with the Great Seal of England. The future colony, however, was most fortunate in the second Lord Baltimore, a brother of George. Cecil Calvert, who had a long, straight nose, piercing dark eyes and a massive jaw, was a practical, farseeing and liberty-loving nobleman whose wife bore the lovely name of Anne Arundel. A county bears her name to this day.

Because Cecil Calvert was much too busy defending his

Leonard Calvert governed Maryland for his brother Cecil.

grant to leave England, he sent over a brother, Leonard, to take possession of the new property and to act as its first Governor.

On February 27, 1634, the *Ark,* a vessel of three hundred tons, together with a much smaller ship called the *Dove,* arrived at Hampton, Virginia, after a long and adventurous voyage that took them to the Canary Island off Africa and to the West Indies. On board was Governor Leonard Calvert, a company of twenty "gentlemen" and about two hundred immigrants.

The leaders were mostly Catholics, as were their free servants. But most of the passengers were Protestant. They too were reliable and honest free men who had been able to pay for their passage and had come "to inhabit and plant" the colony. Each had been promised a grant of one hundred acres for himself, another hundred acres for his wife and the same for each of his children aged sixteen or over. Younger children were allowed fifty acres so a large family easily could own more land than many a minor nobleman back in England. Free servants, whose master had paid their way across the sea, also were entitled to fifty acres of their own.

By chance, Captain Claiborne was present at Hampton when Lord Baltimore's ships arrived, but he stayed apart to avoid causing trouble. In a way this was too bad. The second Lord Baltimore was one of the most intelligent, far-seeing and liberal founders of British America. He knew all about Claiborne's settlement on Kent Island and had given his Governor, Leonard Calvert, wise counsel on how best to deal with Claiborne's claims of independence for Kent Island which lay almost in the center of Lord Baltimore's new colony. Had these two strong men talked, then and there, serious trouble might have been avoided later on.

Among the new Governor's following was Father White and a few other Roman Catholic priests. They were to do a great deal in the years to come towards keeping the Indians friendly and seeing that the promised religious freedom remained a reality.

The Virginia authorities were not at all friendly towards the newcomers. They considered them future rivals in the fur and tobacco trade. Governor Calvert and his colonists therefore lost no time in continuing up the Western Shore.

The first landing they made was on beautiful St. Clement's Island which lies near the mouth of the Potomac River. There they anchored, took on fresh water and explored their surroundings, while their Governor took a small party in a boat and started looking for a more suitable place to plant the new colony.

Leonard Calvert sailed between high, wooded banks up the magnificent, broad Potomac until, near a Potomac Indian town, he chanced to meet three little barks from Virginia. They were commanded by a Captain Henry Fleet who, fortunately for Leonard Calvert, knew this country and its savage inhabitants very well indeed. The Governor persuaded Captain Fleet, a stocky, leather-faced veteran with steely eyes, to join forces. Together, they continued up river till they reached Piscataway Creek.

Spring was in the air and where the Piscataway narrowed, tender new leaves became mirrored on its surface. Multitudes of birds filled the air with song and the marshes smelled sweet with new growth.

All at once the Governor's handful of men became threatened by hundreds of painted and nearly naked bowmen. The Indians ran along the shore shouting threats and waving weapons. But when the visitors made peace talk and offered no hostility they were welcomed by the local werowance. He offered the white men leave to settle on his land: they would have to pay nothing for it.

Governor Calvert heartily thanked the werowance, resplendent in a bearclaw necklace, a belt of wampum—beautiful little seashells threaded together—an otterskin cloak and a tall crown of nodding white swan plumes. Nevertheless in March, 1634, the Governor decided to plant the colony beside the broad, inviting outlet of a gently winding stream which the colonists named St. Mary's Creek. It lay eighteen miles below the land of the friendly Piscataways.

Joyfully, settlers rowed ashore—gentry, yeomen, free servants and indentured immigrants. Captain Fleet wrote:

> We took upon our shoulders a great cross, which we had hewn out of a tree, and advancing in order to the appointed place, with the assistance of the Governor and his associates and the other Catholics, we erected a trophy to Christ the Saviour, humbly reciting, on our bended knees, the Litanies of the Sacred Cross with great emotion.

The new arrivals at once got busy erecting shelters for themselves, their families and the few domestic animals they had

The colonists thanked God for their safe arrival.

brought with them. They decided to call their new foothold
in this great and empty wilderness St. Mary's City in honor
of the Virgin Mary.

St. Mary's was not laid out hit-or-miss to grow in an
aimless way as were most frontier settlements. It was built
according to plans carefully prepared in advance by the
first Lord Baltimore.

Leonard Calvert wrote to his brother Cecil, the Lord
Proprietor: "We have seated ourselves within one-half mile
of the river, within a palisade of one hundred and twenty

yards square, with four flanks. We have mounted one piece of ordnance and placed six murderers in parts most convenient, a fortification (we think) sufficient to defend against any such weak enemies as we have reason to expect here." A palisade was a wall of large pointed logs planted upright in the ground, and the "murderers" he mentions were light swivel guns.

Before any building began Governor Leonard Calvert made a treaty with the werowance of the Yaocomico Indians. He bought thirty square miles of heavily forested territory. This was a trackless tangle but the earth was very dark and rich. It was paid for in part with lengths of brightly dyed cloth, European seeds, hatchets and axes, but mostly with hoes, rakes and spades which these savages, being essentially farmers, were very keen to have.

The settlers could not have arrived at a time more favorable to their project. Their easy-going Wicomoco neighbors had been raided so often of late by the war-like Susquehannocks that they were preparing, when Governor Calvert's ships arrived, to desert their homes and farms in order to move out of the reach of such deadly enemies. Thus the newcomers found quite a few little fields already cleared and some dwellings into which they could move right away.

In exchange for these properties they taught the "naturals" (as the natives were sometimes called) European farming methods and gave them seeds. In return, the Wicomocos and the nearby Piscataways taught the newcomers how best to fish and hunt and how to trade cleverly for beaver and other rich furs which the proud and powerful tribes living farther north had caught.

Also, the local Indians were eager for protection which could be given them by the settlers who carried so many fearsome "thunder sticks"—the Indian name for firearms.

Since the long, hot summer was upon Lord Baltimore's colonists, all manner of food crops were planted as fast as possible, as well as a little tobacco. While tobacco was desirable because it could be used in place of money, the plants wouldn't feed people or their farm animals.

The land was so rich and the climate so favorable that with much hard work bountiful crops soon were shooting upwards. Axes rang and many great trees were felled. Much heavy underbrush had to be cleared away before the first buildings of St. Mary's City could begin to rise.

From the first, the Maryland colonists were determined that they never again would tolerate the injustices and persecutions they had suffered in the home country.

Here in Maryland all free men were to be equal in the eyes of the law after they had sworn fealty to the Lord Proprietor—*not* the King. They could elect some of their number to represent them in a local parliament or Assembly. This body would make the laws under which they were to live. Once a law was passed by the Assembly it was sent to the Lord Proprietor for approval, which he usually granted.

This Assembly of free men who belonged to many religious groups met in 1635, the year after the founding of St. Mary's City.

This was the first example of true democracy in action in North America.

Despite the defenses erected at St. Mary's City, every effort was made to keep the Indians contented by always treating them fairly and by paying for every bit of land needed by the fast-growing settlement.

The infant colony, having got off to a fine start, continued to thrive. One reason for this was that, with so many slow-flowing rivers and creeks in the region, Lord Baltimore's followers could catch all the seafood they needed such as fish of many kinds, crabs, oysters and terrapin. The last is a delicious-tasting brackish-water turtle. In the fall and winter they could kill an abundance of waterfowl almost without effort.

This network of waterways also allowed the settlers to communicate with each other quickly and easily and helped to develop trade. Roads were few and short and would remain bad for a very long time to come.

4 « FIRST HOMES

The first dwellings erected by the newcomers were crude affairs, usually single-room cottages about twenty feet square and framed with crude-hewn timbers just as in New England. To start with, the newcomers made do with chimneys of "catted" clay—clay with oyster shells, reeds and rushes worked into it. Their steep A-shaped roofs would be thatched with reeds from the nearby marshes. The outside walls were protected from the weather by pit-sawed clapboards or "weather boards" as they were called in the south. Often these were nailed onto the frame in an upright position instead of crosswise as was done farther north.

As a rule southern settlers built their chimney outside and against one end of the house. The fireplace of course faced inwards. Often it was so wide that it formed almost the entire end wall. Because stone in that region was scarce and catted chimneys were dangerous, they were built of brick as soon as this material was available.

The usual "first house" had only a few very small windows which were protected by heavy wooden shutters against possible Indian attacks and also against the fierce heat of summer. In the early years glass was very expensive and hard to get, so oiled paper or split animal skins or pieces of horn scraped thin were used in its place. These let in some light but couldn't be seen through. The single door was made of boards heavy enough to withstand serious battering.

The floor would be either of brick laid dry on a thick base of sand or of well tamped down earth. In most cases a small brick oven was also built near the dwelling.

There were not many pieces of furniture in the early Marylanders' homes. Most of the newcomers were very poor and had not been able to bring much furniture with them from England, so they had to make do with benches made of split logs supported by long peg legs set on plain wooden chests or boxes. Sometimes for chairs they used a short length of log with a piece of plank nailed to its back. The table generally would be several rough boards nailed together and then laid across a pair of sawhorses.

Beds at that time must have been most uncomfortable. They consisted of a simple wooden frame crisscrossed by lengths of cord or rawhide thongs. These were used in place of springs to support a mattress filled with rushes, corn husks or, occasionally, dried moss. But the settlers did not complain. They were free and working for themselves at last. Best of all, they could worship God as they pleased.

As months pased without trouble with the Indians, ambitious, bold and energetic settlers and some new arrivals began to venture away from St. Mary's City to take up and clear land in the surrounding countryside. But they still did not go so far that they couldn't run to take refuge behind the palisades in the event of an Indian attack.

Since each freeman had been granted one hundred acres of good land—and much more if he had a large family—

his first task on taking up his new property was to clear away the forest so that he could start growing food crops and a little tobacco for ready money. There were so many trees it was impossible to chop them all down. So the newcomers "girdled" them by cutting off a wide strip of bark all the way around the trunk. This always killed the tree. When the dead trees had dried out the landholder then would start burning over the area. Such fires were supposed to be kept under control with the help of neighbors, but often they got out of control and caused terrible forest fires which destroyed hundreds of square miles of beautiful and valuable virgin forests and drove away game. This loss of a most important source of food made the Indians so angry they sometimes threatened to attack.

When a burnt-over area cooled, the new landowner would plant his first crops between the charred stumps. Later on he would get rid of these nuisances by pulling them out with the help of oxen or by soaking them with saltpetre and then setting the stumps afire.

Out of necessity many home industries sprang up. The women and their older daughters would help to plant and care for flax and vegetables and fruit trees such as apples, pears, cherries, plums and peaches, the seeds of which had been brought from England. This was in addition to doing the cooking and baking and the usual household chores.

They would also make soft soap and dip candles and spin and weave a rough cloth called "homespun" or "linsey-woolsey." Later, when flax became plentiful, the manufacture of coarse linen began. The Indians taught the women how to make dyes out of butternut husks, green walnut rind and sumach berries.

Lord Baltimore wisely forbade his first settlers to spend much time or energy in growing tobacco, so they spent most of their time tending and harvesting such food crops as corn, wheat, rye, oats, squash and pumpkins.

The early settlers grew some tobacco but devoted most of their time to growing vegetables and grain.

A few shaky little wharfs crept out into lovely and unhurried St. Mary's Creek. Soon sloops and barges belonging to traders down the Bay and sometimes dozens of Indian canoes heaped with furs began to tie up to them.

A few ships, most of them small, arrived bringing more settlers from England and Virginia. The population began to increase rapidly. Rough "first houses" went up in all directions and before long many young children could be seen romping about the rutted streets of St. Mary's City. Cattle, pigs and poultry also wandered about freely on the highways.

Everywhere new industries were being started. Saws rasped and hammers banged as skiffs, barges and pinnaces took shape in a crude boatyard. The lumber that went into them came from nearby saw pits. In a saw pit one man stood on a low platform grasping one grip of a long, two-handled saw. He would pull the jagged blade upwards; then his mate, standing in a pit below, would pull it downwards. Between them they sawed a log lengthwise into boards or planks. This was such slow, hard work that soon a water-operated sawmill was built.

Blacksmiths, cobblers, gunsmiths and even a brickyard and a "publick house," or tavern, began to do business.

Male children, as soon as they grew big and strong enough, were put to work tending livestock and protecting it from wild beasts and, now and then, from a roving Indian. Boys helped in the fields, chopped down trees, or cut firewood. Best of all, they liked to be sent hunting or fishing to furnish food for the family.

For quite a while there were no schools of any kind in Lord Baltimore's province. A few of the better-off families, however, did employ a priest or buy an indentured schoolmaster to teach their youngsters to read, write and to do sums.

When the Maryland colony continued to prosper, the wealthier newcomers and ambitious early settlers began to explore various rivers on both sides of Chesapeake Bay— mostly to the north. Such men were seeking a promising location and plenty of rich land on which to lay out and build a great plantation and a manor house. Once they found an area that pleased them they applied to the Lord Proprietor's agents for a grant.

Sometimes thousands of acres were deeded to a single man who had the right connections or was determined to get what he wanted at all costs. On some occasions the new landowner paid as little as a sixpence an acre for some of the richest land in English America. Of course he also had to pay the Indians, but never very much.

5 « ALL SORTS OF SETTLERS

When Governor Leonard Calvert landed at St. Mary's, he had with him some twenty "gentlemen of property" and about two hundred freemen and free or indentured servants, sometimes called redemptioners. These indentured people were temporary slaves. They were of two sorts: willing and unwilling. The willing ones decided in England to sell themselves and their services for a definite period of time in order to pay for transportation to the New World.

As a rule, willing redemptioners were either sturdy people who wished to be free to make something of themselves, or poor but honest people who had fallen onto hard times back in England or who were being persecuted on account of their religious beliefs.

Unwilling redemptioners were either political rebels captured in war or were convicts. At that time the word "convict" didn't mean what it does now. Most of these "convicts" weren't real criminals or hardened felons—of these only a few were brought to Maryland because there was so little demand for them. The "convicts" in fact usually were people imprisoned for debt or small-time offenders against the harsh laws of the time who had been sentenced to prison. In fact the great majority of these unfortunates were plain, not-too-attractive folk desperately eager to forget the past and to make a new start in life. Many poor and uneducated people had been lured to America by the glowing pictures painted by "scawbankers" —disreputable fellows who dealt in the buying and selling of indentures.

The average "convict" redemptioner had his services sold for a length of time equal to the length of the prison sent-

ence he had been given in England. Voluntary redemptioners, on the other hand, deliberately signed themselves into
virtual slavery for a period of about five years. The Maryland buyer of an indentured person would pay about two
hundred dollars for the redemptioner's passage across the
Atlantic. He also promised to protect, shelter, feed and
clothe this temporary slave over the length of his or her
contract. Redemptioners, having absolutely no civil rights,
were completely at their masters' mercy.

Master and man each signed or made his mark on the bill
of sale. When a deal was completed, a copy of this bill, also
signed, was then torn in two. Each man was given a half
which must be fitted together at the end of the term of
service.

At the end of his contract a redemptioner was set free
and granted the right to bear arms, vote and to enjoy all
other civil rights. In addition a newly freed man was given
a few rough clothes, fifty acres of land, an ox, a gun and
some farming tools. A woman on being freed received "a
skirt, a waistcoat of penistone, a blue apron, a linen smock,
shoes and stockings and two linen caps together with three
barrels of Indian corn." At that time these were considered
generous allowances to give the new Maryland citizen a
fresh start in this free land.

It is interesting to note that while Marylanders usually
steered clear of felon redemptioners, they were very eager
to have the services of "convicts" who had been imprisoned
because of religious persecution or for rebelling against the
King of England—as did a great many Scots and Irish.

On the whole, redemptioners were treated fairly well,
especially educated persons such as mechanics, doctors, tu-
tors and clergymen who, though poor, often came from
good families. Frequently, a favored bondsman might be
the younger son of some rich merchant or of a nobleman. If
a bondsman ran away and was recaptured, he sometimes

was forced to wear an iron collar forged about his neck until his service was over.

In all the other English colonies in North America it was lawful to buy, sell and hold captured Indians as slaves, but this never was so in Lord Baltimore's colony. This was another reason why the Marylanders got on so well with the Indians.

When Negroes first were imported to the Tidewater country they were treated like indentured servants who had no limit to their term of service. The holding of Negro slaves as such was not made legal until 1664. The purchase of enslaved Negroes was never popular in Maryland.

6 « TROUBLE OVER KENT ISLAND

Trouble between Captain William Claiborne and Lord Baltimore did not break into flame at once. This was because Governor Leonard Calvert had received wise instructions from his able brother Cecil, the second Lord Baltimore. His orders said he must get the colony at St. Mary's firmly founded and going strong before taking action to gain possession of Kent Island.

About a year after the founding of St. Mary's City, the time came when the Governor was forced into making a move. News had come in that Captain Claiborne's men were arousing the Indians to war. They were spreading a report saying that Lord Baltimore's settlers were not English at all, but were Spanish Roman Catholics who intended to grab the Indians' land and make slaves of them.

This, of course, was completely untrue. It is doubtful whether brave and straightforward Captain Claiborne had any part in putting out such a wicked lie.

Nevertheless Claiborne remained determined never to submit to Lord Baltimore's authority. He kept on trading for furs under the royal license King Charles I had granted him in 1630.

Captain Claiborne sent a pinnace—a small vessel—to "traffick" with Indians living near the mouth of the Pa-tuxent River. The pinnace was called the *Long Tayle* and was the first ship of any size ever to be built on the Eastern Shore of Maryland.

The place where the trading took place was called "Mat-tapony." It lay *only twelve miles* from St. Mary's City!

A journal written at the time describes how business was done.

> Our trade with the Indians for furs is alwaies with dan-ger of our lives. We usuallie trade in a shallop or small pinnace, being sixe or seven Englishmen encompassed with two or three hundred Indians. It is as much as we can doe to defend ourselves by standing upon our guard with our Armes ready & our gunnes present in our handes. Two or three men must looke to the trucke [trade goods] that the Indians doe not steale it, and a great deale of trucke is often stole by the Indians, though we looke ever so well to it.

Alarmed and outraged by Captain Claiborne's bold move so close to his settlement, Governor Leonard Calvert took immediate action. He armed a company of men and sent them marching through great vine- and briar-tangled forests to seize the *Long Tayle*.

Bursting out of sun-dappled woods screaming threats and brandishing their swords, the Marylanders took the Kent Islanders completely by surprise. They captured the *Long Tayle,* her crew and all their trade goods without a fight.

Claiborne's men were taken in triumph to St. Mary's City and thrown into jail. Their pinnace and all the trade goods were confiscated.

When Governor Calvert refused to return Captain Claiborne's property, this tough character seized a Maryland boat in revenge and sailed it back to Kent Island.

Matters got worse when Marylanders sent two armed pinnaces across Chesapeake Bay's broad, clay-colored surface to start trading along the Eastern Shore.

Hearing of this, Captain Claiborne's followers manned a shallop called the *Cockatrice.* This vessel was even smaller than a pinnace. The Kent Islanders were commanded by a tall and handsome young lieutenant named Warren. Under him sailed a crew of thirteen tough, whiskery men wearing pointed iron helmets and somewhat rusty breastplates. They were armed with muskets, pikes and swords. They were determined to stop the Marylanders from trading.

It seems a shame that Englishmen had to fight and kill one another in a great, empty country where there was plenty of room for everybody to be free, and to live and do as he pleased.

Picture an immense, gray-brown river mouth dotted with low-lying islands crowned with dark lines of wind-bent trees. Wide, bright-green marshes laced with pretty, silvery streams and creeks lay in all directions. The Eastern Shore itself was also flat. Tall stands of magnificent pines outlined its shore. Multitudes of waterfowl flew, dived and swam in every cove and river mouth.

Although the *Cockatrice* was smaller than either of the two Maryland vessels, Lieutenant Warren steered straight at his enemies over the choppy water. They levelled muskets and pistols at each other as the distance between the combatants lessened.

The Maryland Commander, wishing to avoid a hand-to-hand fight if possible, ordered his men to open fire at long range. With the first boom, clouds of waterfowl sprang into flight and fled as, for the first time, a sea fight began on Chesapeake Bay.

Despite their enemies' gunfire the Kent Islanders, cheering and brandishing cutlasses and swords, kept sailing through a bank of blinding powder smoke.

When the Kent Islanders came alongside and tried to board, steel clanged and rasped against steel. After a hard fight, Captain Claiborne's hardy followers were beaten back. When at last the *Cockatrice* veered away, Lieutenant Warren and two of his crew lay dead on her rough-planed decking. Only one Marylander was killed in this brief but savage little battle.

Captain Claiborne was enraged over this defeat and appealed to King Charles I to back up what he believed to be his rights. Not willing to wait for an answer from the mother country Claiborne, in a cold rage, fitted out another expedition. It was intended to recover the *Long Tayle* and rescue Kent Islanders still held prisoner at St. Mary's City.

Captain Claiborne was about to lead the expedition himself when letters arrived from his English partners summoning him back to England to make a report on the situation.

Just before valiant Captain Claiborne obeyed orders and set sail for home, he appointed as his successor a smooth-mannered, fast-talking fellow named George Evelin.

At first, acting commander Evelin pretended to be loyal to Captain Claiborne's interests, but soon the rascal slyly entered into negotiations with Lord Baltimore's Governor. He claimed that after looking carefully into the right of the

dispute he had decided Kent Island really did belong to the Lord Proprietor.

Governor Leonard Calvert took immediate advantage of this treachery and sent over a party of twenty well-armed men to take possession of Kent Island in his brother's name.

The invaders surprised and captured without a fight the small fort defending Captain Claiborne's domain.

Cheering and firing salutes, the invaders hoisted the proprietary standard which was Lord Baltimore's coat-of-arms. This design still is the state flag of Maryland. Black, gold, white and red, it remains one of the handsomest and best-designed of all our state flags.

These were very bad times for William Claiborne. On top of all his setbacks in Maryland the authorities in England told him his license to trade was no longer in force. Nevertheless that stubborn gentleman refused to give up. Grimly he prepared to wait for the right time to recapture his beloved Kent Island. Claiborne could not foresee that he would have to wait nearly fifteen years for that moment to come.

Naturally the settlers at St. Mary's City were relieved and overjoyed by the capture of Kent Island. At the same time they were beginning to realize that the winning of true and permanent freedom was an uncertain and often dangerous business.

Waterfowl took flight and fled, as the first sea fight on Chesapeake Bay began.

7 « THE COLONY TAKES ROOT

As more and more land was taken up along both shores of Chesapeake Bay, the number of simple homesteads increased rapidly. Already some of the ramshackle first houses had been added onto. More often, a bigger and more comfortable dwelling went up close by. The old first house sometimes was used as a barn or to house a redemptioner if the landholder really was getting ahead.

Immigrants who landed at St. Mary's City knew they would have to face many hardships, but they didn't mind. So long as they were free to rule themselves locally and to worship God in any way they pleased, no danger or discomfort appeared too great.

For a time it seemed that serious trouble with colonies planted by other European nations could not be avoided. In 1650 the Dutch under a Captain Mey established a settlement, Fort Casimir, on land claimed by Lord Baltimore in what now is the State of Delaware.

Then Swedes under a leader named Johan Prinz, who "weighed upward of four hundred pounds and drank three drinks at every meal," took Fort Casimir away from the Dutch.

Before long the Hollanders recaptured their fort and held it until Dutch power in North America ended when New Amsterdam (New York) was captured by the English in 1664. There was never any fighting between the Marylanders and their foreign neighbors although they came close to it on several occasions.

For two reasons the Province kept growing at a healthy rate. First, because the trade in rich and silky-smooth beaver skins and other valuable furs was booming. Second, now that the settlers had become better established and had all they wanted to eat, they were able to devote more time and energy to the planting of tobacco.

Some Marylanders were becoming really well-to-do for, as has been said earlier, during those early days in the Tidewater country of Maryland and Virginia, tobacco took the place of cash. Debts, taxes, land and labor could be paid for with it. All prices were reckoned in pounds of tobacco.

Even government officials were paid off with "hands" of tobacco. A hand consisted of five leaves of cured tobacco tied into a bunch which very much resembled a human hand. The best tobacco grown was a variety called "oronoko," so for a long time, small but successful tobacco planters were nicknamed "Oronookos."

What few metal coins there were in circulation often got hacked into four pieces called bits to make change. Hence the phrase: "That will cost you two bits." This chopped-up coinage was also called sharp money because the sharp edges on the bits cut holes in people's pockets.

The vast expanse of Chesapeake Bay gradually became dotted by more and more little vessels and boats with such colorful names as pungies, bugeyes, skipjacks and sharpies. Skiffs and dugout log canoes followed lazy, winding creeks and rivers ever deeper into this land of lovely, lush countryside that bordered Maryland's countless waterways.

Since the growing of tobacco called for much land, a new landowner would build his home near the middle of his holdings, and so he would have no near neighbors. Villages were few and far apart and grew only slowly. But since no really big wars had been fought in that part of British America and only a few plagues had struck, the population of Maryland kept on growing.

Thanks to encouragement from the Lord Proprietor's agents, enough food crops were being raised to feed everybody. In ever-growing numbers nimble, black-and-brown pigs and lean cattle roamed the woods. In order to prove

Because everyone on the lower Chesapeake travelled by water, ship building was an important industry.

ownership, settlers notched their livestock's ears in distinctive fashion.

Because roads were still few and very bad, horses did not come into great demand until a little later on. On the lower Chesapeake everybody still travelled by water whenever possible.

Crude but necessary industries expanded. Boatyards began to go up everywhere. With abundant fine timber right at hand, shipwrights did a thriving business in building small

and medium-sized vessels. Most of these craft were ugly but sturdy and serviceable.

Once a bondservant had completed his term of service he usually claimed and staked out the fifty acres due him on liberation. As a rule the land granted to an ex-redemptioner was either well up a stream or in the depths of a forest.

A free man now, he became another of many small-time planters who were beginning to form the real backbone of Lord Baltimore's colony.

As soon as the newly freed man had put up a shelter against the weather he would start clearing his land with the help of an ox he had been given on receiving his freedom. This done, he hopefully set about planting his first crop. The land was so fertile—two feet deep of rich black soil—that the freeman planted tobacco wherever he could.

If he was smart he soon began to make money, for in a favorable market the "sot-weed" (as tobacco often was called) brought as much as five shillings a pound! Small planters, like the Oronookos, had only to sell a few hogsheads of good tobacco before they were well on their way towards security.

Mister Oronooko then would look about for a wife—often an ex-redemptioner like himself—to keep his home and give him children. Eventually the youngsters would help him in the tobacco fields. Next he would buy more land.

If Mr. Oronooko continued to do well he would buy the contract of an indentured man such as he himself had been. Sometimes, after a few years of successful planting, he was able to buy the services of several redemptioners and become a man of real importance in the growing community.

Since all tobacco was shipped by water, the new planter always tried to obtain land as near to a stream as possible. At first this was easy. There was plenty of land for everyone, but later on tobacco, which required a lot of space, began to be planted on clearings located farther and farther away from the nearest creek, bay or river.

To serve such plantations, what were known as "rolling roads" had to be built. Great casks of tobacco thus could be rolled overland to the closest wharf. These strongly constructed casks were nearly as large in diameter as a man. To move them, temporary axles were fitted to frames built about the round container. The cask then could be pulled down to the water by a span of patient, slow-footed oxen. Generally, the planter and his men would push from behind for often these early rolling roads were very rough in places.

With credit obtained through the sale of his tobacco, Mister Oronooko was able to buy tools, seeds, weapons, and labor, and even a few comforts for his increasing family.

All metal had to be imported from England. Pig iron was in great demand. It could be forged by the plantation's blacksmith into tools and other necessary hardware. As yet there were no foundries in Maryland.

Bricks also were needed, but they did not have to be imported. There was plenty of suitable clay right at hand. Bricks were formed in what was called a "pugmill" and fired in a furnace at the brickyard. From the start, very fine bricks were made in Maryland.

As more small planters prospered they grouped into loose-knit, widespread communities. They seldom built

Great casks of tobacco were pulled along "rolling roads."

their homes close together in hamlets or villages for mutual defense, as was done farther north. So long as the Indians remained friendly there was no need to do this.

In the Tidewater country food was so plentiful that from the earliest days Marylanders prided themselves on their hospitality.

So comfortable was the living—humble enough according to our present-day standards—that more people came flocking in. They were very keen to settle in Maryland.

8 « CAVALIERS AND ROUNDHEADS

Things in Maryland were going well when, on the other side of the Atlantic, a terrible political storm blew up in England. This broke into a dreadful civil war which threatened to limit or end many of those precious rights and liberties Marylanders had struggled so hard to win.

Backed by a Protestant sect called Puritans, the English Parliament had rebelled against the so-called divine right of kings. In practice, this meant that a king could rule his country just as he pleased. His ordinary subjects had little or nothing to say about how the government was run.

The Puritans claimed they were fighting for freedom against the King's tyranny and in a way they were. But victory for the rebels would threaten the precious civil and religious liberties granted in 1632 by King Charles I to the first Lord Baltimore.

These rebels against the King sometimes were termed

Charles I had granted religious and civil liberties to the first Lord Baltimore.

Oliver Cromwell's victory forced people of different religions to flee to the New World for sanctuary.

Parliamentarians. The armed forces of the Puritan party were called Ironsides. For the most part the rebels were a grim, humorless lot who believed that *their* way of winning salvation in heaven was the only way. They would kill or savagely persecute anyone who disagreed with them.

The Ironsides were led by Oliver Cromwell. He was very capable but merciless.

After a long and bloody war that left many a prosperous town and proud castle in smoking ruins, King Charles I was defeated and captured. Later he was condemned to death. On a gray morning in 1649 he was led out of a window in one of his palaces onto a platform. There a grim figure wearing a black mask and holding a broad-bladed axe in his hands stood waiting beside a block. The King was very brave and forgave his enemies before quietly laying his head on the block. A moment later he was beheaded. For a time the royal power in England was at an end.

After the execution of King Charles I, a freely elected representative government took power. This was named the Commonwealth and was headed by Oliver Cromwell. He was called the Lord Protector.

Without mercy, Cromwell and his principal followers, nearly all of whom were Puritans, continued to persecute anyone who disagreed with their ideas. The Irish suffered especially.

Roman Catholics, Church of Englanders, Quakers, Methodists and members of many other Protestant sects fled either to Europe or to the New World. A great many of these refugees chose to seek "the Land of Sanctuary" in America.

These were dangerous times for Lord Baltimore and for the rights of the people he was trying to protect.

Being a wise man, Cecil Calvert never came to his Province but stayed in England and "bent with the wind" in order to protect the unusual rights granted under his

Charter. For the first time he appointed a Protestant, William Stone, to be his Governor in Maryland. From the very beginning, Governor Stone had a hard time.

There was much unrest in Maryland because people feared that the Commonwealth government would cancel Lord Baltimore's Charter and take away the religious and political freedoms which to them were as dear as the breath of life.

Most unhappy of all were Maryland's Catholics. They were hated both by the Cavaliers (Royalists) and the Roundheads (Parliamentarians). Supporters of the Commonwealth were called Roundheads, because they wore their hair cut short above the ears in a "Dutch cut" instead of wearing it shoulder-long.

About this time trouble again was caused by Captain

Cavaliers and Roundheads both hated the Catholics.

Captain William Claiborne fiercely defended Kent Island but was merciful to his enemies.

William Claiborne. A staunch Cavalier himself, he secured the support of the Royalists, who had remained strong in Virginia. He then revived his claim on Kent Island.

At the head of one hundred grimly determined soldiers, stubborn Captain Claiborne and another leader named Bennett appeared before St. Mary's City. They ordered George Stone, who was governing under Lord Baltimore's authority, to submit. Governor Stone tamely surrendered.

After what had been done to him back in 1636, this victory for William Claiborne was sweet revenge on the Lord Proprietor.

Although determined and forceful, hawk-faced Captain Claiborne was also merciful. To his eternal credit he took no revenge whatever on the men who, as he claimed, had robbed him of his holdings on Kent Island.

Lord Baltimore was furious over Governor Stone's failure to fight. All the same he reinstated Stone on condition that Lord Baltimore's name as "Lord Proprietor" appear on all commissions, writs, claims and other official papers issued by his government.

This angered a large number of Puritans who had been welcomed to "the Land of Sanctuary." They had fled from England after King Charles II had mounted the throne and had driven out the Roundheads.

In 1654 Captain Claiborne got together with some Puritans and decided to depose Governor Stone for a second time. On this occasion Governor Stone was braver and prepared to maintain Lord Baltimore's authority. He assembled a force of about a hundred tough, well-armed men. Putting his troops in a number of blunt-bowed pinnaces and shallops, he sailed to attack the Puritans at Providence. This was a stronghold established by them near the entrance to the lovely, quietly flowing Severn River.

Captain William Fuller, who commanded an almost equal force of Puritans, sallied out boldly to attack Governor Stone as soon as he had landed. Captain Fuller had the advantage of having a small man-of-war, the *Golden Lion,* to back up his troops.

It is easy to picture the bloody little battle which followed. The two forces, in ragged lines abreast, advanced towards each another over a wide and level meadow. This was bounded on two sides by Spa Creek, a pretty little stream flowing into the Severn River.

With brightly colored ensigns and standards waving above them and with sunlight gleaming on their weapons, the two forces steadily drew closer together.

Musketeers carrying matchlock muskets blew on their slow matches till they glowed yellow-red and were ready for instant use. Soldiers who were armed with wheel-locks made sure the clockwork mechanism of their weapons was wound up tight.

Many soldiers wore morions, or pointed iron helmets

that sometimes had a nasal, or nosepiece to protect the wearer's face. Dented breastplates flashed here and there amid the opposing ranks. Neither side wore uniforms. Some were roughly dressed in baggy breeches of some coarse material, others had on leather knee pants. Many wore striped or ragged jerseys under jerkins—sleeveless coats—of thick cowhide. All were dirty, bearded or unshaven except, perhaps, some of the officers.

When the tramping fighters came in range of each other they began to yell ringing battle cries. The Puritans charged, shouting: "In the name of God fall on! God is our strength!" Lord Baltimore's men yelled back: "Hey for St. Mary's! Come on ye rogues! Ye Roundhead dogs!"

Firearms began to bang and roar; swords, pikes and daggers glittered on the sunlit meadow as the two forces became locked in deadly, merciless combat.

There sounded breathless shouts, bellowed orders and howls of pain. Soon the shooting died out. Musketeers had no time to reload. In those days reloading a firearm was a very slow and complicated business.

The battle was being fought without much advantage to either side until the *Golden Lion* came sailing up Spa Creek and fired a broadside into the rear ranks of Lord Baltimore's followers.

When they found themselves attacked from behind, the Lord Proprietor's men broke and ran. Almost all of them were killed, wounded or captured, except a very few who escaped by swimming across Spa Creek to woods on the far side.

Governor Stone was captured and condemned to death, and would have been executed if some Puritan soldiers hadn't protested. Although Stone was spared, other prisoners were hanged without trial from nearby trees.

The battle on Spa Creek ended with Cavalier Captain

Claiborne and his Puritan allies in full control of the Provincial government, but again he took no personal revenge on those he thought had robbed him of Kent Island.

While all this was going on, Cecil Calvert, the second Lord Baltimore remained in England. Although he dearly wanted to, he never saw his American property. Skilfully, he kept on fighting to save the special rights and privileges granted under the Charter (sometimes it was called a patent) to his father.

Cecil Calvert was successful.

In 1658 the government of Maryland was returned to the Lord Proprietor and Claiborne's claims were again denied.

Captain Claiborne returned to Virginia. He was brokenhearted but lived to the ripe old age of ninety. This happened very rarely in those rough and brutal times.

In the years that followed there were many changes in the government of England. Cromwell died and was succeeded by his son who soon was overthrown by a revolution which restored the Stuart Kings of England to their throne. After King Charles II died, James II came to the throne. James II in turn was driven out in 1688, and William of Orange, a Dutch Prince, became King as William III. He was married to Queen Anne who had inherited the throne of England. Queen Anne, who had been born a Danish princess, was beautiful and gracious and clever as well.

A new settlement, located on the Severn River near where the battle on Spa Creek had been fought, was at first called Anne Arundel Town. This new town grew quickly because it was better situated than St. Mary's City for carrying on the all-important tobacco trade—which was still the colony's greatest source of income.

About this time King William III took away the power to rule from the Calvert family. He made Maryland into a Royal Province—like its neighbor, Virginia.

For a time Cecil Calvert remained Lord Proprietor in

name only. He had been reduced to a landlord ruling in the King's name. Now, neither he nor his settlers had much to say about what went on in Maryland.

The first Royal Governor was Sir Lionel Copley, a crotchety and narrow-minded old man who governed the Province for only two years before he died. During that brief time, however, he brought about a number of changes in the Land of Sanctuary. For the first time Marylanders were forced to pay taxes directly to the Crown. They also were required to pay the Governor's salary and that of other Royal officials.

Lord Baltimore and his followers in America bitterly resented this loss of their rights. It has been said that the first seeds of discontent—which ended with Maryland's joining in the American Revolution—were planted by the laying on of these taxes.

Governor Copley also made the Church of England the official church of the Province. Every free man was ordered to pay forty pounds of tobacco a year to support the new state religion.

Worst of all, the Royal Governor abolished the right to religious liberty in Maryland.

About the only good thing Governor Copley did during his short term in office was to create a small squadron of armed vessels. This was the first Coast Guard in North America. Its main job was to suppress smuggling and to drive off pirates and buccaneers who came sailing up from the West Indies. These outlaws raided the American coast from Florida to New England. When they entered Chesapeake Bay they would capture small unarmed ships. Often they murdered a whole crew.

Sir Lionel Copley was succeeded by Francis Nicholson, who was commissioned by King William III. Governor Nicholson, arriving in 1694, ordered the Maryland Assembly to meet at Anne Arundel Town on the Severn. Almost immediately afterwards, this thriving little settlement was renamed Annapolis in honor of Queen Anne and made capital of the Province.

Annapolis was blessed with a much bigger and deeper harbor than that at St. Mary's City. Long since, the original settlement had ceased to grow. Many of its inhabitants, searching for new land, had moved farther north or sailed over to settle on the Eastern Shore.

In response to the Governor's summons, Assemblymen hailing from all parts of Tidewater Maryland began to arrive. Mostly, these locally elected representatives came by water. The killicks (crude anchors made of stones enclosed in a wooden frame) of quite a few battered, brown-

Puritans settled on the banks of the Severn.

sailed little boats were dropped in the still largely empty harbor of Annapolis.

Still, there were not very many representatives. Some eighty years after Governor Leonard Calvert had established the first foothold at St. Mary's, barely twenty-five thousand white people inhabited Lord Baltimore's Province.

Nevertheless, some owners of these ungainly little craft showed signs of becoming well-to-do. Quite a few merchants and small planters turned out in handsome, well-cut clothing made in Europe. Most of the Assemblymen, however, were still far from genteel or fashionable in their appearance. Wearing floppy, wide-brimmed hats, they were bearded, sunburned and sturdy. They seemed to be always on the alert. Some carried a tomahawk or a cutlass in addition to a pistol or two slung in a wide leather belt.

The raw new capital's few unpaved and puddled streets were thronged with colorful types. There were red-faced, hawk-nosed Royal officers in gold-laced and often brilliantly colored military jackets. They tramped about town with gold-mounted swords sticking out behind like a dog's tail. A few gentlemen wore shoulder-long, unpowdered but carefully curled wigs under flat-crowned black hats decorated with white or brightly dyed ostrich plumes. Flemish lace, usually torn and dirty, showed at their wrists and cascaded down their shirt fronts. Big silver buckles gleamed on their footgear.

By contrast, the Oronookos and small merchants mostly wore coats of butternut-dyed homespun, white thread stockings and breeches made of leather grown shiny through long use.

Moving about with a loose-kneed stride were a few Representatives wearing brimless fur hats made of fox, coon and possum pelts. Their loose-fitting hunting shirts were fringed about the hem and around the shoulders. These hard-eyed, bearded fellows carried scalping knives and tomahawks and looked about as if they expected to glimpse a painted savage crouched behind every rock and clump of bushes. These men lived in the backwoods or along the wild frontier above the headwaters of Chesapeake Bay.

When the Maryland Assembly met for the first time at Annapolis, it was in the home of Major Edmund Dorsey, a leading citizen. His large, brick dwelling still stands on St. George's Street.

One of the first things the Assembly did was to try to fill a serious gap in the development of Maryland. Governor Nicholson and his Council urged that: "A way be found out for the building of a free School for the province and a maintenance for a schoolmaster, and usher, and a writing master, that can cast accounts: The which, if it can be agreed upon, his Excellency proposes to give fifty pounds towards building the said school and twenty five pounds Sterling a year towards the maintenance of the masters during his Excellency's time."

The Assembly also voted to establish a kind of circulating library for the benefit of soldiers defending lonely little forts and blockhouses far from civilization. This was a worthy but hardly a practical idea since most enlisted men and many officers of that time could neither read nor write.

For a time, things went fairly smoothly for King William III's Governor. Nevertheless, the Marylanders were quietly plotting to regain the unusual political and religious privileges they had enjoyed in the past.

Governor Nicholson was a principal founder of Annapolis. He hired a professional architect to draw plans for the new capital. The town was to be laid out in sections. One was for the homes of the gentry, another for those of trades-people. Districts were set aside for warehouses, shops and wharfs. Set well apart were areas for such unpleasant-smelling trades as fish curing, tanning, brewing, dyeing and the slaughtering of animals.

9 « THE END OF ROYAL GOVERNMENT

Towards the end of the seventeenth century, Marylanders became aware that great tracts of unsettled land belonging to the Lord Proprietor of Maryland lay to the north and west of the head of Chesapeake Bay. This wild, heavily timbered and often very rugged country had a harsh climate very different from that of the lush, low-lying Tidewater.

In still largely unexplored western Maryland lay a succession of very high hills and mountain ranges. The Blue Ridge range is one of them. These ran roughly northeast and southwest. In this wilderness lived a number of fierce and powerful tribes, among them the Shawnees, the Miamis, the Iroquois and other equally unfriendly savages. Rightly enough, they feared that the arrival of pioneer families would drive away the game on which Indians depended for food, clothing and shelter. The savages therefore lurked in ambush and used tomahawks and scalping knives on any whites they came across.

This part of Maryland was and still is very beautiful country. It has many lovely, softly rounded hills and mountains covered with blue-green woods. Fast-running, icy-cold mountain streams splash down rocky gorges. Rapids roar whitely over shallow places. Heavy snow covers the land from November till April. In the extreme western part of the Province not much land was suitable for farming, but northwestern Maryland was very rich in furs.

The European market was hungry for beaver and other fine furs, so increasing numbers of courageous and hard-bitten frontiersmen, mostly of Scottish and Irish origin, began trapping in Maryland's mountains. Soon a few widely scattered blockhouses and fortified trading posts were built amid the great and silent forests. But there were still no settlements of any importance.

To the foothills and lowlands below the Alleghanies came another type of settler who mostly wanted to farm. Many of these people were Germans. Others were former redemptioners or religious refugees who had fled Europe.

Tough and resourceful, these pioneers, like the hunters and trappers in the mountains, soon learned how to deal with the Indians who hated their coming. If they failed to learn, they soon were parted from their scalps.

The frontiersmen of northwest Maryland at this time were too few to secure direct representation in the Assembly at Annapolis. Nevertheless, these pioneers formed a very valuable part of Maryland's population because, gradually, the English colonies were beginning to touch hands all the way from New England to the Carolinas, and such people provided contact with their neighbors.

When rich deposits of iron ore and other valuable minerals were discovered in the wilderness, several small foundries and blast furnaces began to operate near the head of Chesapeake Bay.

About this time two small but bitter frontier wars were fought: King William's War, which lasted from 1689 until 1697, and Queen Anne's War, which raged from 1702 until 1713. In New England these conflicts were called the First and Second French and Indian Wars. Both were waged to keep the French in Canada and their Indian allies from invading and conquering the English colonies.

Fortunately for Maryland, the very powerful Iroquois Six Nations chose to fight on the English side. For a long time these ferocious warriors were kept so busy to the north that they seldom found opportunity to take the warpath as far south as Chesapeake Bay.

With considerable help from their American colonies, the English won both of these wars. Nevertheless, the

French decided to build a line of forts and trading posts throughout what is now called our Middle West. This line was nearly two thousand miles long and stretched all the way from Detroit down to Mobile on the Gulf of Mexico. Such French outposts would remain a menace until the third and greatest of the French and Indian Wars broke out in 1755.

Maryland, not being directly threatened, sent no troops and only a few volunteers to help beat back the French and Indians. Grudgingly, the Lord Proprietor's people did send a few "free gifts" to support the colonies farther north.

As huge tracts of land were given over to the planting of tobacco, a lot more labor was needed, but by this time the trade in indentured persons had almost come to an end. Planters, desperate for labor, now began to purchase Negro slaves. Luckily, they didn't need anywhere near as many as were brought into Virginia and the Carolinas where the growing of rice and cotton called for a much larger force of laborers.

Because there was danger of capture by pirates or French men-of-war during the wars mentioned above, the colonies for a time imported Negroes directly from Africa instead of through the West Indies. It was only with reluctance that Maryland planters bought these unhappy black people. But, as they saw it, they had to or go broke.

Tobacco quickly exhausts the soil in which it is grown. If too many crops were planted on the same piece of ground the soil would wear out and become useless. Since the use of chemical fertilizers was unknown, there was a great and ever-increasing demand for fresh land. Great wooded areas, often quite far from water transportation, had to be cleared and cultivated by crews of Negro slaves toiling all day long under a hot sun.

In February, 1715, Charles Calvert, third Lord Baltimore, died. He was the only one of all the six Lords Proprietor who actually lived on his American property—and he stayed only a year. He owned Maryland, but when the Province was made a Royal Colony, he was robbed of the right to rule personally over his beautiful and prospering colony.

He was succeeded by his Protestant son, Benedict Leonard. Benedict became the fourth Lord Baltimore but died only two months after his father.

His son, Charles, became the fifth Lord Baltimore. He also was a Protestant and was only sixteen years old.

Rule over Maryland by Royal Governors ended in 1714 when George I, a German Prince from Hanover, succeeded William and Mary to the throne of England. Because George I was a Protestant, he promptly restored to the Fifth Lord Baltimore the powers, privileges and liberties that had been taken away from the Lords Proprietor.

The Calvert family then ruled Maryland almost as independent princes until just before the American Revolution began.

PART TWO

GOLDEN DAYS ON THE TIDEWATER

10 « FIRST TASTES OF FINE LIVING

Once the Lords Proprietor had had their governing powers restored, Marylanders felt free to devote their main attention to peaceful tasks. However, it was still necessary to think about protecting their northern and western frontiers. A good many pioneers had begun to take up land and settle in the little known wilderness above Chesapeake Bay.

In that area they lived in constant fear of French-led Indian attacks. Any day, at any hour a painted war party, whooping and waving tomahawks, might rush from dark and gloomy woods to wipe out little settlements or to massacre garrisons and burn down weakly held outposts.

To protect the frontier a line of three strong log forts was built between the Patapsco and the Susquehanna Rivers.

To man these defenses, a company of Rangers was recruited. The Rangers usually wore black leather skull caps, perhaps decorated with a fox's or a coon's tail, green-dyed linen hunting shirts and fringed Indian leggings. These hardy fellows were armed with tomahawks, big knives and, whenever possible, with sure-shooting, long flintlock rifles.

All Rangers had to be tough, resourceful and expert in the Indian style of fighting. They were so efficient that other colonies quickly copied their organization and methods. Such units became known as rifle companies or regiments. As will be seen, they fought bravely and well all through the French and Indian Wars and later in our War for Independence.

Now that the population of Maryland had increased to over 60,000 white people and about 12,500 Negro slaves, little settlements began to spring up to the north of a thriving new settlement called Baltimore Town. It was located at the mouth of the Patapsco River. Baltimore Town was incorporated in 1729.

One must understand that the word "town" at this time did not necessarily describe a large community. Any place in which lived twenty men capable of raising a riot could call itself a "town." Under the law, if twenty or more men started to make trouble, a senior magistrate was called upon to "read the Riot Act" and order the troublemakers to scatter.

Baltimore Town, more centrally located than either St. Mary's City or Annapolis, was better placed for traffic with the interior. Also it had a magnificent harbor which could handle the largest ships then afloat.

Slowly but steadily Baltimore Town attracted domestic and foreign seaborne trade away from Annapolis. But the provincial capital remained for a long time the wealthiest, handsomest and most important town in Maryland. St. Mary's City was falling into decay and soon would cease to be of any importance. Farsighted Tidewater Marylanders continued to take up big holdings inland where the soil was fresh and unspoiled.

We have seen how very crude the first homes were. Now, handsomer and more substantial dwellings began to rise along the Tidewater country's rivers, creeks and bays.

These better homes built by Oronookos—the local term, it will be recalled, for successful small planters—were called Big Houses. These dwellings were very much like small

Baltimore Town was small and centrally located and had a magnificent

harbor, which could handle even the largest ships of the time.

English manor houses. Always constructed of well-made red brick, they usually stood two storeys high. Some had an attic on top.

The typical Big House had only two large rooms on its ground floor—a living room and a dining room. These were separated by a hallway which ran all the way through the house. At one end of this hallway would rise a more-or-less elaborately carved wooden staircase. The second floor was wholly taken up with bedrooms. There were no closets, only wardrobes, since even well-to-do people didn't own many clothes at that time. Perhaps there might be a tiny bedroom or two in the attic. Nobody liked using them for they were icy cold in winter and stiflingly hot in summer.

Furniture for the new Big House was still fairly scarce. What there was was very plain except for a few fine pieces imported from Europe. The climate in the Tidewater country was so mild that Marylanders could spend much more time out-of-doors, and thus did not need as much furniture as their northern neighbors.

Standing near to the Big House would be a cluster of small, whitewashed wooden buildings. The closest would be the kitchen. Because of smells and long periods of very hot weather, cooking always was done outside the family's living quarters. The kitchen generally was connected with the main dwelling by an open breezeway. Later on this passageway was enclosed.

The other out-buildings would include a plain, brick structure in which Mister Oronooko did business and kept the plantation's accounts. Then there would be a storehouse in which food and other supplies for the main dwelling were stored. Another building was a small one intended to house the overseer or one of the landowner's married children. Often such a dwelling might be the planter's original first house.

Since these new homes always were built close to or on

a waterway, a dock, long enough to reach deep water, jutted out from the shore or river bank. Over this dock hogsheads of tobacco could be rolled right aboard a waiting vessel.

Little attention was given to the planting of decorative flower beds. Gardens were only for growing food or herbs for medicines.

At some distance from Mister Oronooko's fine new brick house, a clump of rough shacks would be put up to house redemptioners and a slowly increasing number of Negro slaves. This group of shelters came to be known as The Quarters.

Still farther off stood a number of well-ventilated barns in which valuable tobacco leaves could be stored and cured in a variety of fashions.

If the planter had selected his homesite with care, he would build, nearby, a low stone- or brick-lined springhouse in which icy water could curl around crocks containing dairy products and other perishable foods.

Plenty of cured meat was always available. This meat might have been smoked or pickled or dried. Another way to preserve meat was to cook it and, while it still was hot, to cram it tight into an earthenware crock. A deep layer of melted fat then was poured in to seal out air. Finally, a tight-fitting lid was fixed onto the crock. Nobody knew why this method worked, but it was a fairly good means of preserving meat.

In addition to homegrown grains, vegetables and fruits, an unlimited supply of oysters, crabs, fish and terrapins that thrived in "salt rivers" were always at hand to grace the table.

Once spinning and weaving became common, all linen cloth for the plantation was made from flax grown right at home. This cloth invariably was dyed blue before being cut and sewn by slave labor into garments for everybody.

Since very few sheep were raised along the Tidewater, it

was necessary for Mister and Mistress Oronooko to import woolen cloth or ready-made garments either from England or one of the northern colonies. In Maryland, cotton cloth was not yet in common use.

Mistress Oronooko had other duties besides running the house and bringing up her flock of children as best she could. Since there were very few white doctors around and none of them much good, she also acted as doctor for the little community. If someone fell really sick, a slave would be sent running to fetch the nearest Indian medicine man.

At that time vaccination was unknown so a great many people died of smallpox. Those who survived generally were badly pockmarked and disfigured for life. George Washington was one who suffered from this disease.

When someone suffered from a bad tooth, a travelling barber would be paid to yank it out. If such a barber wasn't available, the plantation blacksmith would take a pair of pincers and, causing screams of pain from the victim, extract the aching tooth. Alas, this brawny, blackened fellow didn't *always* pull the right tooth! Few people had many teeth left by the time they were thirty years old.

Babies and young children died in great numbers for lack of even the simplest medical knowledge.

Because death struck early and often, men and women in all classes of society got married as many as five times. This was necessary because there always had to be someone on hand to help the surviving mate rear an always increasing swarm of young ones. Families of twelve and fourteen youngsters were by no means uncommon.

An industrious small planter got up at dawn and went downstairs to drink a mug or two of home-made beer brewed from corn. Few apples were grown in Tidewater Maryland so cider was not available.

After drinking his "eye-opener," Mister Oronooko wiped his mouth, mounted a horse and rode out over dew-spangled fields with a grownup son or his overseer—if he was rich enough to have one—to inspect the state of his crops and find out whether his field hands were on the job.

Around ten in the morning the planter returned home for a hearty breakfast of spoonbread (a stiff pudding made of white cornmeal), vegetables, beef, turkey, pork or some other kind of meat. Eggs were quite scarce for, in those days, hens were bred mainly for eating and not for laying eggs.

He would then probably go to his office to attend his plantation's accounts, write to agents about selling his tobacco or perhaps figure out what he would need by way of supplies.

Dinner (lunch) was generally served between three and four o'clock in the afternoon. In summertime supper was eaten around nine o'clock, after the evening cool had set in. In winter the last meal of the day was placed on the table while the sun was setting.

The appearance of cheaper and better guns made it easier than ever for an Oronooko family to enjoy plenty of big and small game all year round. Sometimes hunters favored the use of a light crossbow which, being silent, did not scare game away after a first shot had been fired.

As a small planter prospered, more out-buildings would go up around the Big House. There might be a larger spinning house, more extensive stables, a smokehouse and enlarged blacksmith's and carpenter's shops. These last two crafts were about the most important in the successful operation of a plantation. Probably the last out-building to be built would be a modest frame schoolhouse. Not much thought, time or money was wasted on it. Children were of more use in the fields than studying books.

While life in the Tidewater country was growing steadily more comfortable and secure, quite a few lonely little cabins and stations began to dot the forests and plains of northern and western Maryland. A station consisted of a few fortified

The Oronooko families enjoyed game all year round.

log cabins (they were called strong houses) built close together and connected by a palisade of logs.

A salty, fearless and able frontiersman named Thomas Cresap built the first blockhouse on the Susquehanna River. Captain Cresap was nicknamed "Big Spoon" because of his generous hospitality to all comers—white or Indian. A large and energetic man, he had an eagle's beak of a nose and deepset, bright blue eyes. He had learned the grim business of fighting Indians so well that, early on, he became a leading figure in the defense of Maryland's northwestern frontier. As we shall see, some of Tom Cresap's many sons also became famous as fighters, first against the wild and dangerous Indians and then against the British.

About this time clashes took place between the Lord Proprietor and the heirs of William Penn. Penn, another Proprietor, but with less power than the Calverts, had founded Pennsylvania about forty years after the *Ark* and the *Dove* had anchored in the St. Mary's River.

Charles Calvert, the Fifth Lord Baltimore, was vain, bad tempered and not very bright. He had allowed himself to be tricked by a map wrongly showing the boundaries of his Province. Maryland thus lost 2,250,000 acres to Pennsylvania and 1,500,000 more to Delaware on what is now called the Delmarva Peninsula. This last includes the entire Eastern Shore of Chesapeake Bay.

A definite, mutually agreed upon boundary had never been established between the two Provinces so, without warning, a force of Pennsylvanians moved in to take up land they claimed as theirs. They burnt Captain Cresap's house, killed some of his men and wounded the Captain.

Captain Cresap was taken to Philadelphia where he looked about and said coolly, "Philadelphia is the finest city in Maryland."

Through the use of tact and forbearance on both sides, further bloodshed in this boundary dispute was avoided.

To settle the Maryland-Pennsylvania boundary for all time, a pair of English astronomers and mathematicians named Charles Mason and Jeremiah Dixon were brought over from the mother country. They camped out, suffered dreadfully from the weather and from hunger, and were in constant danger of attacks by savages.

Mason and Dixon took four years—from 1763 to 1767— to complete their survey across raging rivers and through often mountainous wilderness. Their work was very accurate. Modern surveys reveal that Mason and Dixon rarely erred by more than two or three feet in deciding the boundary between Maryland and Pennsylvania. They drove this line westwards through the wildest sort of country for a distance of two hundred and thirty miles. They could not survey the boundary as far as had been intended because the savages drove them back.

To fix their line they placed stone markers a mile apart. Once in every five miles they planted a larger "crown stone" bearing the coat-of-arms of Lord Baltimore on its south side and that of William Penn on its north side. To make the line even more distinct, trees and underbrush were cleared away for a distance of about fifteen feet on either side.

Although war had not yet been declared between England and France, the French kept the fierce northern Indians so stirred up that in New England, in Pennsylvania and in western Maryland they often went on the warpath. These small raids left settlers just as dead as if they had perished in a big battle.

When such Indian attacks became more frequent and deadlier, the Maryland Assembly voted to fortify their principal towns. Baltimore Town for a brief time became the only walled city in the whole of British America.

Two gates in the pointed palisades allowed plain country folk, riding in creaking two-wheeled carts and lumbering

A Mason-Dixon boundary stone on the Maryland-Pennsylvania border.

farm wagons, to enter the town along with the varnished coaches and bright carriages of politicians and rich men. This wall didn't last long. During a severe winter three years later it was pulled down and used for firewood.

Fortifications of a sort also were raised to protect Annapolis and Frederick Town, which was becoming the most important settlement in western Maryland.

11 « THE OHIO COMPANY

In 1749 a very important event in the early history of Maryland took place. King George II of England deeded the rights for half a million acres along the Ohio River to a group of influential Maryland and Virginia merchants, planters and politicians. This organization was known as the Ohio Company. The granting of this land was to trigger a great war which lasted almost twenty years and, around the world, cost many thousands of men, women and children their homes and lives.

To keep out settlers sent by the Ohio Company, the French, who also claimed the Ohio Valley, built forts on Lake Erie and on the big Miami River. Also, they called in great hordes of bloodthirsty Indians from Canada by promising them as much loot and as many scalps as they could take. The French King's officials were determined to kill off all the English colonials or to drive them into the sea.

To find out the true situation, Governor Nicholson of Maryland sent an enormously able and fearless frontiersman named Christopher Gist on a mission to the Miami, Shawnee and Delaware Indians who felt their hunting lands were being threatened. Gist's deep-set, burning brown eyes were so dark in his deeply tanned face that they appeared black. We will soon hear more about Christopher Gist.

During this winter expedition into the dark and tangled wildernesses of the Ohio Valley, we catch our first glimpse of a big-nosed young surveyor named George Washington. Then twenty-two years old, he stood well over six feet tall in his stockinged feet and was very broad shouldered. His hair was auburn and his eyes were a clear, piercing steel-

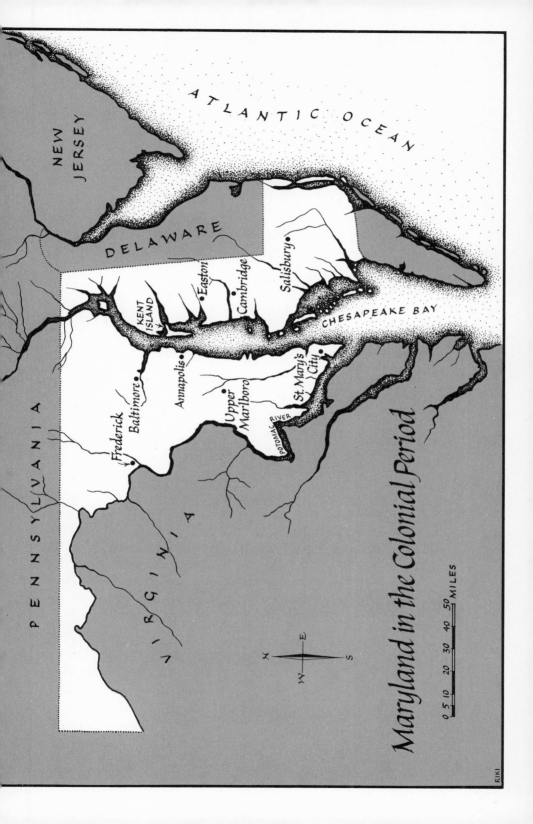

Maryland in the Colonial Period

gray. Captain George Washington had been sent by Governor Dinwiddie of Virginia on a mission very like that of Christopher Gist.

After joining forces, Washington and Gist approached the hard-bitten and experienced French authorities at Venango in eastern Pennsylvania. They warned them to stop causing trouble and to pull their troops and savage allies out of the Ohio country.

Haughtily, the French commander refused. He then stirred the local tribes into a bloodthirsty frenzy by spreading a rumor that the English were about to take away their hunting grounds.

Both sides began to prepare for a bitter life-or-death struggle.

12 « THE ORONOOKOS GO TO TOWN

Two or three times a year Mister and Mistress Oronooko would make a shopping trip to the nearest town of any size. Sometimes they and their family travelled in a fast little sailboat which might be handsome enough to be called a yacht, but more often they went to town in a battered, unpainted little tub generally used for hauling freight.

If their shopping place lay fairly close at hand, the Oronookos went to market in a stout barge rowed by four or six brawny Negro slaves. The travellers shielded themselves from the sun or rain under a canopy raised in the stern. However, if their destination lay inland, a pair of rough-coated and broad-backed horses would be hitched to a farm wagon or a crude carriage. Laughing and frolicking, the whole family would pile in to go bumping and jolting over the owner's rolling road until it joined a rough track leading to the local seat of trade and government.

Probably Mister Oronooko and his older sons would ride on horseback ahead of the wagon with guns balanced across the pommels of their saddles. They kept a sharp lookout whenever the unpaved road passed through woods or skirted one of the many gloomy and snake-filled swamps in the vicinity. A few sad-eyed hunting dogs would jog along beside them or under the wagon.

If any Negro slaves were to be sold, these would trudge along after the cart with hanging heads and despair in their hearts. Their hands were bound only if they had run away or had proved dangerous.

On the road the Oronookos were likely to meet friends and neighbors—people very like themselves who were travelling in the same direction. The prospect of going to town was really exciting for all the family. Living on a small plantation located far up some lonely little river was often a dull existence.

Probably the Oronookos would stay with friends or relatives during their visit to town. This was because the "ordinaries" or taverns of that day were small, dirty and noisy. It was nothing for patrons to sleep, fully dressed, with three or four strangers in a bed full of bugs and fleas. A few fussy innkeepers insisted that people remove their boots before going to bed.

Once shelter had been found, Mistress Oronooko and her wildly excited or painfully shy children started shopping from a list prepared over many weeks. Eagerly, they inspected new merchandise in various shops. The older daughters chattered, flirted and showed off new clothes—if they had any.

Boys and young men preferred to hang around the blacksmith's forge or look yearningly at the gunsmith's wares. Some preferred to attend horse and livestock sales. They also liked to brag with others of their age about the fine hunting and fishing to be found on their father's plantation. Naturally they boasted a lot about what fine hunters and shots they were.

If court happened to be sitting, there would be added entertainment. Who knew but that some hangdog offender might not be marched out amid hoots and jeers to be locked into a pillory or stocks standing in front of the jail, or perhaps in front of the courthouse itself. More serious criminals, stripped to the waist, were bound to a post and severely whipped. Others were branded with a red-hot iron on the ball of the left thumb with a letter *T*. Now and then some wretched fellow would be hanged.

Female wrongdoers usually were punished by ducking.

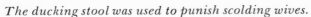

The ducking stool was used to punish scolding wives.

Tied onto a stool fixed to the end of a long pole, the poor woman was lowered again and again into cold water. Often she half drowned. If her offense was very serious, she might be whipped.

For Mister Oronooko this jaunt was far from being a mere pleasure trip. He had serious business to attend to. Supplies of many kinds had to be bought for the months ahead. Sometimes he purchased or sold a slave or two. Or he might dicker for some piece of land adjoining his holdings. If he bought property, the deed had to be registered in the courthouse.

The planter also had his say about proposed laws and the election of representatives to the Maryland Assembly. Sometimes he sat on a jury.

Mistress Oronooko, after she had bought what she needed, visited friends, drank tea and exchanged gossip; all the time she kept an eagle eye out for likely suitors for her marriageable daughters.

Only after all his business had been completed would Mister Oronooko set about amusing himself. Plenty of attractions beckoned this hard-working man. There would be more-or-less impromptu horse races, bouts at cudgels, wrestling matches and tossing the iron bar to be watched and wagered upon. After the sun had set, he most likely would find his way to a smoke-filled tavern where he could gamble, swap tall stories and probably drink too much. In those days it was not unusual or considered shameful for men from all walks of life to get so dead-drunk they would have to be carried home by friends.

13« THE "TOBACCO ARISTOCRACY"

By 1750 there was no doubt that, man for man, Maryland had become the richest of all the British colonies in North America. Although tobacco still was king, lands suitable for growing wheat had been found recently to the west of Baltimore Town and near the frontier settlement called Frederick.

Every year the business of smelting pig iron was growing more important. The first pig iron from Maryland had been shipped to England in 1718.

But tobacco-growing southern Maryland and the Eastern Shore remained by far the most prosperous sections of the Land of Sanctuary.

By now quite a few great plantations covered hundreds, even thousands of acres. When their owners grew very rich, they put on airs and became what plain Marylanders called Big Wigs or The Tobacco Aristocracy.

Some of the most successful planters were descended from people who had come to America in the *Ark* and the *Dove* or aboard ships which had arrived at St. Mary's City shortly afterwards.

More of these "nabobs" (a Hindu term for a powerful or wealthy man) were heirs of redemptioners who, through hard work, intelligence and sometimes ruthlessness, had made the most of that freedom which their ancestors had come to seek in Maryland.

Among this elegant class were many aristocratic relatives and friends of the Lords Proprietor and their Governors. These gentry had fallen in love with the rich and beautiful Province. After pulling up roots in the old country such aristocrats took up as much land as they possibly could.

Other members of the Tobacco Aristocracy were influential men who had come to Maryland from other British colonies in America to escape harsh, unhealthful climates or to enjoy religious freedom. Many more came to escape the constant danger of destruction by the French and Indians.

Having decided to build himself an impressive manor house, the successful tobacco planter would explore his property in search of a site suitable to his new needs. On some occasions when the location couldn't be improved upon, the ambitious, newly rich landowner added onto the Big House built by his Oronooko ancestors. More likely, however, he would tear down the house in which he had been raised and would start afresh. He would import a well-trained architect, landscape gardener and skilled artisans from England to plan, erect and beautify his new dwelling.

Almost always the fine new home was built to face some lovely creek, bay or river. Because most of these great houses were built during the reigns of Kings George I and II, the style became to be termed Georgian.

Squire Big Wig's new manor house was always constructed of well-made, native-fired red brick. Many were tastefully ornamented with elaborately carved wooden pillars, shutters and other white-painted trimmings.

One of two main doors faced the water and sometimes the plantation's dock. The other opened onto a circle at the end of the estate's main driveway. This circle was rimmed with carefully clipped boxwood, yews or some other evergreen shrub. Sometimes the driveway leading to a Big Wig's house was a mile or more in length. More often than not, a double row of shades trees was planted along its length. These level and gleaming white roadways were made of crushed oyster shells.

Elaborate formal gardens, handsome shubbery and well-pruned hedges surrounded Squire Big Wig's new home.

The settlers' lives grew more elegant with prosperity.

Close to the manor house was planted grass imported from England. Sheep were kept to graze on the lawn and keep it short and velvety, for even a well-swung scythe could not shorten it more than three inches.

To protect this precious lawn from damage by straying stock, a "ha-ha" often was built around the manor house. A ha-ha was a low brick wall built along the bottom of a shallow ditch. A ha-ha could not be seen from the house but it did keep out farm animals.

In the manor house, there were elegant ballrooms, clev-

erly designed staircases, dining rooms beautifully panelled
in yellow pine, game rooms and parlors furnished with
fine furniture, crystal chandeliers and oriental rugs. Such
luxuries were bought for Squire Big Wig by his factor (business agent) in London, who shipped them to the New
World at great cost.

Pewter or wooden tableware no longer was seen. Gleaming, solid mahogany tables now were set with delicate
French porcelains and china. Candelabra, tableware of
solid silver and crystal goblets sparkled and shone in mellow
candle light.

Quaint or informative names often were given to these
great homes: Sophia's Dairy, Araby, Bachelor's Hope, Duck
Pye, Punk Neck, Charles' Gift and The Devil's Wood Yard
among others.

Amusing names are to be found in ancient Eastern Shore
graveyards. No doubt some of these were adopted by ex-
"convicts" and redemptioners who wanted to forget the
past. Imagine choosing such a name as James Wildgoose,
James Tendergrass, Thomas Halfpenny, Peter Blackboard
or Ringing Bell!

On a great plantation might live two thousand or more
souls, important and humble, free and slave. In the course
of time such a vast property became all but self-supporting.

The only drawback to life on the great estates was that
they most often lay many miles apart from each other. When
the Big Wig family went visiting, it was not to spend only
a weekend with friends and relatives but to stay for weeks
and even months!

No traveller, no matter what his condition or occupation,
ever was turned away from the manor house. Hospitality
was so generous that quite often members of the Tobacco
Aristocracy went broke trying to match some richer neighbor's generosity ("keeping up with the Joneses," as we say
nowadays).

Many amusements were enjoyed in and around a manor house. There were lavish dinner parties, parlor games, balls and less formal dances. Quite often the mistress of the house and her daughters entertained guests by singing or by playing on a spinet imported (from Europe) at considerable expense.

There were many entertainments for men. During the cold months the host and his guests could go wild fowling or deer hunting. Fishing was enjoyed all year round. The sport of fox hunting, too, was growing popular, especially in the rolling countryside around Baltimore Town. English-bred foxhounds and thoroughbred hunters were to be found on many great estates. Horse racing and the breeding of racers became a passion with many Big Wigs. There was also bowling-on-the-green, archery, croquet and card playing to amuse less energetic guests.

Perhaps the most colorful and the favorite sport of that period was tournament tilting. After several small wooden hoops had been hung from a crossbar, a young buck—often they called themselves "knights"—would mount a favorite horse, level a lance and, at a full gallop, try to run it through a hoop and tear it free. He who freed the most hoops gained the right to name his best girl "The Queen of Love and Beauty." In some parts of Maryland tilting tournaments are still held each year.

There were special celebrations for Christmas, Easter and Whitsunday (the seventh Sunday after Easter). Everyone on the plantation, white or black, took part.

The Negroes particularly enjoyed Christmas. It was a very old tradition that no work was to be done by anyone—except house slaves—while the Yule log burned. It was suspected that, before the slaves brought a Yule log to the manor house, they had soaked it so thoroughly it would burn very slowly indeed.

14 « THE BIG WIGS VISIT THE CAPITAL

By the middle of the seventeenth century Annapolis, capital of the Maryland Province, had grown into a handsome and sizeable little city. Annapolis was busily entering what was called its Golden Age.

Many of the Tobacco Aristocracy had begun to build elegant town houses in Annapolis in addition to their great manor houses in the country. They competed fiercely with each other to see who would own the finest home in the Provincial capital.

They were able to indulge expensive tastes without much trouble because ships carrying tobacco in one direction and European-made goods in the other now sailed directly between Annapolis and England. In growing numbers slow, bluff-bowed merchant ships imported the latest styles in furniture, dress, literature and speech. As more and more Big Wigs established homes in the capital, Annapolis became a hub of culture, business and politics.

Squire and Mistress Big Wig, bored with their isolated life in the country, would linger as long as they could to enjoy the brilliant social life. During the fall and winter, many balls and beautifully prepared dinner parties were given. Celebrated artists performed at many of these entertainments or at least graced them with their presence. Guests were treated to the finest wines and liquors which could be imported.

The streets of Annapolis were gay with scarlet, gold-laced uniforms and the brightly colored coats of men wearing the latest styles from London. Men who followed the latest fashions were called "macaronis," or dandies. As a rule these splendid, white-wigged gentlemen would carry an ele-

gant, often bejewelled, walking sword—for show only, as it
was of no use in fighting.

Styles in women's dress did not change so often or so
noticeably as they did for men. Mistress Big Wig nevertheless felt it important that she be dressed in the latest mode.
There were no fashion magazines. Instead, dolls called
"fashion babies" were dressed in the latest London styles
and sent to shops in America for display.

Women still dressed their hair simply. They drew it
straight back from the forehead and tied it in a loose knot.
Some younger women left a few curls to either side or
allowed a long, carefully curled "lovelock" free to dangle

Squire and Mistress Big Wig enjoyed leisurely Sundays.

over a shoulder. Then the hair was powdered by a maid. On her hairdo, Mistress Big Wig usually wore a little frilled cap.

Bodices stiffened with stays of whalebone were worn tight. Often so much of the lady's neck and chest was left bare that she made use of "modesty pieces" of lace or lawn across the top of the bodice. As many as four or five lace-trimmed petticoats were worn beneath the lady's fine overskirt. This was to keep the wearer's legs and lower body warm. "Panties" then were unknown. Hoops of various design made skirt and petticoats flare out prettily.

When a fashionable gentleman chanced to meet a lady of

his acquaintance, he would "make a leg" (a very deep bow). The gallant then would sweep off his ostrich-plumed or gold-braid-trimmed hat and sweep his headgear across the ground before the lady as if brushing dirt from her path.

Fancifully carved and gilded four-wheeled chariots and coaches were drawn by four or six lively horses wearing shining, silver-mounted harness. They were driven by very solemn, bewigged black servants wearing colorful livery. Grandly, such coaches would sweep past wheelbarrows, humble two-wheeled carts or some farmer's cart drawn by slow-footed oxen.

If they were going only a short distance in town, the gentry rode in glass-enclosed sedan chairs. These chairs often were decorated by painted garlands and roly-poly cupids and were carried by two Negro slaves in splendid uniforms.

Several gentlemen's clubs had come into being. One, the Tuesday Club, had been established as early as 1745. There was no clubhouse but members met by turn in each others' homes. The South River Club established in 1772 is still in existence and claims to be the oldest social club in North America.

In November, Squire Big Wig and his friends enjoyed a "meeting" or a series of horse races held on the new race track just outside of Annapolis. Many gentry came from surrounding colonies to enter horses they had raised. George Washington was one who attended several times.

The first real theater to be built in British America was erected in Annapolis about this time. It was called the Temple of Thespis.

There were other less pleasant amusements such as dog-fights, bull-baiting and cockfighting on which large sums of money were bet.

It must not be supposed that the plainer citizens did not have their own sports and amusements. They did a great deal of folk dancing such as had been done in England for centuries. There were also wrestling matches, fisticuffs (boxing), cudgel and quarterstaff bouts with a money prize and plenty of beer and rum to drink.

One of the common people's favorite pastimes was a turkey shoot. In this cruel sport, the bird was placed in a pit with only his head sticking up above from behind a log. As the turkey seldom kept still it was a very difficult mark to hit. Sharpshooters also fired at a wooden target from considerable distances. These contests were generally won by leathery, quick-eyed Rangers and rawboned, big-bearded men from the backcountry.

Even by this time only a few public schools had been established in all Maryland. King William's School for Boys had graduated quite a few classes. Education was supported by a penny tax on tobacco. Before long, King William's School for Boys became a full-fledged college. Today it is known as St. John's College in Annapolis.

It must not be imagined that the Tobacco Aristocracy did nothing but amuse themselves during their visits to Annapolis. Sales of tobacco had to be negotiated and orders prepared to be filled by Squire Big Wig's agents in England. Also, there was important legislation to be discussed.

Many Big Wigs and their wives became annoyed by the fine airs adopted by Englishmen who had come to America to serve Lord Baltimore's government. They, and officers of the King, tended to look down on even the most cultured Marylanders. They called them "beastly Colonials" simply because they hadn't heard about the latest styles and gossip.

This attitude started a growing dislike of homegrown Englishmen. It would increase by leaps and bounds when King George II sent some of his regular troops to America to fight the French and their savage painted allies.

In spite of such minor irritations, these were glorious, memorable days for the Provincial capital. Few of the gay, worldly and witty people in Annapolis paid much attention to black war clouds gathering to threaten Maryland's northern and western frontiers.

15 « THE THIRD FRENCH AND INDIAN WAR

The threat to Pennsylvania, Maryland and Virginia in the establishment of a strong French fort on the present site of Pittsburgh—Fort Duquesne—was too great to be tolerated. An army of one thousand four hundred British regulars and four hundred and fifty Colonials was sent to destroy it. While the whole army was commanded by General Edward Braddock, the Colonials, with quite a few Marylanders among them, were led by Lieutenant Colonel George Washington.

They set out from Alexandria, Virginia, for Fort Duquesne in the blasting heat of summer. The regulars suffered terribly because of their thick woolen coats of scarlet and the heavy equipment they carried. Insects and thirst also bothered them. The army advanced only very slowly through high, densely wooded hills because they had to build a road to accommodate wagons which General Braddock insisted on bringing along.

In vain did Rangers and old frontiersmen like Christopher Gist warn of Indians swarming and skulking unseen in the woods. There were also white-coated French officers and men among them. The enemy numbered about nine hundred men in all.

About seven miles below Fort Duquesne the road they were building was jam-packed with red-coated soldiers wearing white cross belts, which made them excellent targets. Part of the army already had crossed a river they were following in the wake of a scouting party guided by Christopher Gist. The rest were preparing to cross when suddenly a volley of musketry rang out. Frightful, gobbling scalp yells rang through the hot air.

The troops ahead halted as men began to fall, and the

British became confused. Wanting to shoot, they fired blindly but did little damage.

It soon appeared that the redcoats were nearly surrounded and were allowed no room to fight in the European manner —in well-ordered ranks. They knew nothing about falling flat or taking cover.

Washington begged permission to take some Colonials and infiltrate the woods but was refused by General Braddock, who shortly afterwards was mortally wounded. All the time the musketry was deafening. Screeching Indians pounced on men who tried to break out of the tangled mass of red-coats.

Then the ammunition ran out, and bayonets under these conditions were useless. Regulars who had begun slowly to retreat were at least covered to some extent by Colonials flitting about and firing from behind trees.

The carnage continued until nightfall while the wounded groaned and implored help which never came. Next morning, Braddock was dead and with him well over half his army, among them not a few Maryland volunteers.

All the colonies were shaken to the core by the ghastly massacre which has been called The Battle of the Wilderness but is better known as Braddock's Defeat. They and the mother country grimly set about repairing the damage and preparing to defeat the French once and for all.

Fortunately for all concerned, William Pitt, the British Prime Minister at that time—1759—was honest, shrewd and forceful. He sent to America the best ships, troops and generals he could spare, although the Seven Years War was raging in Europe.

Fortunately for Maryland none of the terrible battles that followed took place on her soil, nor were any Maryland troops involved.

What Pitt planned was a three-pronged attack on the

French in America. One small army he sent to capture Fort Niagara, another to drive up the Hudson River and Lake Champlain. The latter was to take the French forts at Crown Point and Ticonderoga.

The third force was a combined army and navy operation. Its job was first to seize the great French naval base at Louisburg, and then to continue up the St. Lawrence and conquer the capital of French Canada.

The first expedition succeeded in its objective by capturing Fort Niagara.

The second striking force, however, was unsuccessful because the general in command ordered a frontal attack on veteran French regulars occupying a great, stone-walled "Star" Fort at Ticonderoga. He was repulsed with such ghastly losses that the French took heart. But for all that, they soon were forced to blow up their own forts and retreat toward Quebec.

The third assaulting force, divided into two armies, was brilliantly successful. One was under the command of Major General Jeffery Amherst ("a soldier of the King"), the other led by Brigadier General James Wolfe. With the help of the Royal Navy, the latter took Louisburg and then stormed Quebec in September of 1759.

This ended the French threat forever and the English-American colonials could live in peace, but only after thousands upon thousands of lives had been lost, countless settlements had gone up in smoke, and a vast fortune—for those days—had been spent.

It was the problem of how to pay for this war that soon was to cause an ever-widening separation between the colonies and the mother country.

Maryland volunteers were among those who went down to defeat with General Braddock.

PART THREE

FORGING "A FREE AND INDEPENDENT STATE"

16 « RETURN TO A RAVAGED LAND

Although the Third French and Indian War had ended with the capture of Quebec, it went on in Europe and on other continents until 1763. Abroad, this was called the Seven Years War.

Now that French power had been broken, survivors of the people who had fled eastward after General Braddock's terrible defeat began to return to their homes along the frontier. With them went many new pioneers who took up holdings in western Maryland. Among these were many German Lutherans who had escaped religious persecution in Europe.

They were sober people, hardworking, devoted to liberty and to their adopted country. Being mostly farmers they cleared a great deal of forest land. Before long, rich valleys along the Monocacy River and Antietam Creek glowed with billows of golden wheat and corn.

The harvested grain was hauled east by oxcart to be ground into flour at the Ellicott brothers' mills near Baltimore Town. The Ellicotts had been the first to prove that land which had become worn out through too much planting of tobacco could be made suitable for growing wheat. They brought shiploads of "paste" (lime) down from Nova Scotia in Canada and plowed it into lifeless earth. In the pleasant, rolling country around Baltimore Town and on the newly cleared lands not far south of the Mason-Dixon Line, fine harvests began to be reaped.

In the mountainous wildernesses of Maryland's westernmost part, brave and hardy men started trapping and trading again. Although the "old French War" had been over for some time, this was still a mighty dangerous way to make a living. Many Indian tribes had returned to their old hunting grounds. They were determined to keep the white men out at all costs.

Backwoodsmen and their families had to be tough to live as they did in crude and uncomfortable one-room cabins. Such cabins were made of logs notched in the Swedish fashion—for it was the Swedes who first imported to America the art of building a house of logs. The timbers had their ends cut off so enemies couldn't climb them.

Backwoods families lived under crude conditions.

After the walls had been raised, roofs made of slabs of bark were lashed down onto a framework of poles. Chimneys built of sticks and clay smoked badly and often caught fire. Although a chinking of chips, clay and moss was mixed together and driven in between logs placed one on top of the other, plenty of cold air still leaked in. More cold breezes beat in through loopholes cut to enable a pioneer to shoot at attacking Indians.

The families generally wore fur hats and garments of tattered homespun or of stiff, often patched deerskin. Rarely did the frontier people wear underwear or stockings. There was no running water or plumbing of any sort. All the family's hair hung in lank, greasy strands and seldom got washed.

An axe being about the only building tool available to many backwoodsmen, their carpentering work was pretty rough. As in the early days on the Tidewater, all articles in daily use, such as plates, cups, spoons, forks and dippers, were whittled out of wood.

Despite these hardships the population of western Maryland increased rapidly. Settlements such as Frederick, Hagerstown, Westminster and Cumberland became towns in the modern sense. Within ten years there were enough people living in northwest Maryland to elect and send representatives to Annapolis to make their wishes known in both Houses of the Maryland Assembly.

Baltimore Town, incorporated in 1729, began to become really important. It was the natural seaport outlet for the products of farms and mines lying inland. Soon more and more ships from England and from the other American colonies came to Baltimore's good-sized harbor rather than to Annapolis.

In 1763, a chief of the Ottowa tribe named Pontiac, who was also a medicine man, organized a great alliance of

Indian tribes from the Gulf of Mexico to Canada. He intended to drive all white men into the sea.

This conspiracy, as it was called at the time, was poorly organized, but eight out of twelve British outposts were captured along a thousand-mile front. Their little garrisons often were slaughtered to the last man.

The conspiracy failed along the southeastern frontiers of Pennsylvania, Maryland and Virginia when Colonel Bouquet, a Swiss mercenary and a veteran Indian fighter, led some Maryland and Virginia militia into the Indian country and beat the savages on their home ground. The defeated Indians were driven far back, but western Maryland suffered badly all the same.

17 « THREATS TO LIBERTY BEGIN

King George II died in 1760 and George III started one of the longest reigns in history.

King George III thought his American colonies unable to defend themselves, so he sent over ten thousand British regular troops to garrison the frontiers and crush Indian attacks like Pontiac's conspiracy. To transport, arm and supply so many troops was a costly business. Besides, debts left over from the French and Indian War still had to be paid.

To help meet these expenses the King's ministers decided to tax the colonies. That was when real trouble between the colonies and the mother country began.

With passage of the Stamp Act, as this tax was named, a mighty roar of protest went up from Georgia all the way to New Hampshire. The colonists held that King George III's ministers were trying to force on them a tax which was illegal because it had been imposed without the knowledge or consent of the colonial governments. Marylanders were especially outraged. Under their charter, they had been promised they would never have to pay taxes *directly* to the royal government.

The tax itself was small. A few pennies was the cost of a stamp which had to be stuck onto all newspapers, pamphlets, official documents and the like. This tax also had to be paid on playing cards and dice. It was not the price of the stamps but the idea behind them which raised such a storm. When stamp distributors tried to sell the hated bits of paper they were threatened, tarred and feathered, hanged in effigy and actually beaten up in Annapolis and other ports.

Next, the King's ministers ordered the Writs of Assistance. This allowed officers of the law to enter a man's home with a blanket search warrant which had been issued on secret information.

After that came the Navigation Act. This placed high tariffs (taxes) on cargoes either coming from or going to the mother country, and prevented the colonists from trading *directly* with any foreign country. If they wanted to ship goods, say to Holland, the ship carrying that cargo first had to touch at a British port and pay duty.

The American colonists decided to take combined action. A congress, nicknamed the "Stamp Tax Congress," met in New York. Representatives from Maryland conferred with delegates from eight other colonies. Christopher Gadsden struck a keynote by saying: "There ought to be no New England man, no New Yorker, no one on the Continent, but all of us Americans."

Angry colonists gathered to burn stamps as a protest against unfair taxation.

This unified effort brought results in England. In March, 1766, the hated Stamp Act was repealed by Parliament.

Nevertheless, the King's Prime Minister, Charles Townsend, continued to plot to gain control of colonial governors and judges. He also ordered that certain kinds of prisoners must be brought to England for trial. This was against colonial tradition.

On top of all this, Townsend's government decided to place a tax on many articles exported to America from the mother country. Among these goods was tea.

Again the colonists protested. Seeing that recognition of their rights could not be won by words alone, they began quietly to collect arms, ammunition and other warlike supplies. Underground military units who called themselves the Sons of Liberty were formed. They held drills in secret. Committees of Observation were appointed to keep an eye on what the royal government might be up to.

Before the unified defiance of the American colonies the King's Ministers again backed down. They lifted the import tax on everything except tea. Trade was resumed with the mother country and for a while things went better.

It was the tax on tea which brought matters to a head. In the colonies tea was a very popular drink; coffee then was little known. Some members of the British government who owned shares in the East India Company ordered that tea should be forced upon the colonists.

Ships bringing in tea were made to turn back from Philadelphia and New York. In Charleston, South Carolina, the tea was allowed to be landed but no one would pay the tax to buy it, so it was held in a well-guarded warehouse. Patriotically minded colonists drank "liberty tea," which was made of dried raspberry leaves.

In Boston, three ships bearing tea were kept tied up for nearly a month before a party of young patriots dressed themselves like Mohawk Indians and one night boarded the ships. Screeching and yelling, they split open the tea chests and dumped them into Boston harbor. This colorful but highly illegal raid was called the Boston Tea Party.

News of this defiance of the Crown spread like wildfire throughout Britain's American possessions. A British official in Annapolis wrote, "All America is in a flame! I hear strange language every day. The Colonists are ripe for any measures that tend to the preservation of what they call their natural rights."

The Boston Tea Party being deemed an act of rebellion, the King sent more troops to Boston and ordered the port closed to all commerce.

Maryland at once sent a message of sympathy to Boston. Then came her own turn to defy the Crown.

In Annapolis an overseas trader named Captain Anthony Stewart owned a ship called the *Peggy Stewart*. She reached Annapolis in October, 1774, almost a year after the Boston Tea Party. Among the *Peggy Stewart*'s cargo were several chests of tea.

When the local Committee of Observation heard about this, a mob led by some Liberty Boys raised a gallows in front of Captain Stewart's house and threatened to burn his home down if he did not destroy the ship which had brought in the tea. The mob became so menacing that Captain Stewart decided he'd better row out to his ship and set it on fire.

While a great crowd along the shore looked on, dazzling tongues of flame began to lick out of the *Peggy Stewart*'s ports and hatches. Fire roared up her well-tarred rigging, took hold of the sails and sent burning rags and glowing brands flying far out over the water. Giving off great clouds of smoke and steam, Captain Stewart's tea ship burned to the water's edge and sank.

In spite of all this, the royal government stubbornly refused to lift the tax on tea. The colonies therefore decided

From an upper window of this house, Anthony Stewart's wife and daughter watched the burning of the Peggy Stewart *and her cargo of tea.*

not to trade with the mother country in any way—only among themselves.

Everyone expected that after the *Peggy Stewart* had been destroyed King George III would send troops to Annapolis and close the port as he had done in Boston. But this didn't happen.

It is an age-old principle that the best way to conquer an enemy is to divide his strength by getting him to quarrel with his friends and allies. The King's Prime Minister cunningly thought to split apart the rebellious Americans by going easy on the southern colonies while treating the northern colonies with harshness.

When this scheme failed, King George III dissolved the Virginia House of Burgesses—a governing body rather similar to the Maryland Assembly. At once a call went out for all colonies to send delegates to another General or Continental Congress which was to meet in Philadelphia. Maryland sent eight representatives. Only Georgia of the thirteen colonies did not send delegates. This Congress sat from September 5 to October 26, 1774. The delegates worked hard to get together and make plans for the future. They also advised inhabitants of all the colonies to arm and form their own militias. The representatives agreed to assemble again in May, 1775, in Philadelphia for the next Continental Congress.

But slow progress was made in recruiting troops and collecting enough military supplies.

A Maryland Convention assembled in December, 1774, at Annapolis. To it came eighty-five delegates representing all the counties of Maryland. This Convention passed several important resolutions. Among these was a promise to support Massachusetts to the utmost in her struggle against the Crown. Maryland also offered to help *any* colony threatened by illegal taxation or the use of royal troops.

The Convention further voted to establish: "A well-regu-

Eighty-five delegates attended the Maryland Convention in Annapolis.

lated militia composing gentlemen, freeholders and other free men, which is the natural strength and only stable security of a free government." This resolve provided that male inhabitants of Maryland from sixteen to fifty years of age could be called on to form militia companies. To this provision was added a rather sly argument: "Such militia will relieve our Mother Country from any expense in our protection and remove the pretense . . . of taxing us on that account." To arm the militia, money was voted for buying weapons and ammunition.

A conference was held between a committee appointed by the Maryland Convention and officers of the Lord Proprietor and the royal government. Nothing came of these sincere efforts at reconciliation.

On April 18, 1775, a sharp little battle was fought between non-uniformed Massachusetts Minute Men and the King's Troops. The redcoated regulars had marched out proudly from Boston with flags flying and drums rattling to destroy some military supplies collected by patriots in Lexington and Concord.

It shows how very bad communications were that news of this small but very important military clash did not reach Annapolis until April 28, and this was supposed to have been record speed for express riders! We who live in an era of smooth, straight expressways, with bridges over every creek and river, can have no idea what it was like to travel over muddy, crooked roads, to ford streams, or to risk one's life on rickety little ferries which ran only once in a while, or not at all in bad weather.

Immediately, the Maryland Convention sent a committee to call on the Governor, Robert Eden. It demanded that all arms, ammunition and other military supplies belonging to the Lord Proprietor or to the Crown be placed in the hands of patriotic organizations.

The Second Continental Congress assembled in the State House (later it would be called Independence Hall) at Philadelphia. On June 15, 1775, Thomas Johnson of Maryland nominated George Washington to be Commander in Chief over all troops raised by the United Colonies. Washington was unanimously elected.

The Congress was in session when a breathless messenger flung himself off a lathered horse and dashed inside bearing the thrilling news of the Battle of Bunker Hill. This bloody struggle had also taken place on June 15, 1775.

After attacking three times with stubborn bravery, the British finally had been able to drive American militia—who had run out of gunpowder—from their positions. The King's troops were victorious, but they paid so ghastly a price that a British officer commented sadly, "Another victory like this and we shall have lost the war."

Now that the chips were down and war had begun, the United Colonies—as they now called themselves—really got busy. They started collecting troops to help Massachusetts keep the British forces penned up in Boston. Congress ordered American ports thrown open to the world. A post office department was authorized. Congress also established a Treasury Department which began to print lots of paper money. Benjamin Franklin became our first Postmaster General.

For her part, Maryland hurried to raise two companies of light infantry. The first company was commanded by Captain Michael Cresap, another son of "Big Spoon," the old Indian fighter. Such was the magic of the Cresap name that riflemen travelled a hundred miles and more to serve under a member of that famous family.

Cresap's men were burning for action and very eager to march to Cambridge, Massachusetts, where General Washington already had taken command of the Continental Army, as the loosely united militia from several colonies had become known.

In Virginia, Daniel Morgan, a survivor of General Braddock's terrible defeat, enlisted a similar company of riflemen. The Virginians were just as keen as the Marylanders to start shooting "Lobsterbacks," as the British were called on account of their bright red coats. The two units started a friendly race to see who could reach Boston first.

When they passed through Philadelphia, a gentleman described the appearance of the rifle companies: "I have had the happiness of seeing Captain Michael Cresap marching at the head of a formidable company of upwards of one hundred and thirty men from the mountains and backwoods, painted like Indians, armed with tomahawks and rifles, dressed in hunting-shirts and moccasins."

Apparently the race to Cambridge ended in a tie, for Cresap's and Morgan's riflemen marched together from Cambridge to the siege lines on Dorchester Heights overlooking Boston. These lean, leathery men were welcomed with cheers, patriotic speeches and, one suspects, plenty of good New England rum.

A Mr. Thacher wrote: "They now are stationed on our lines, and their shots have frequently proved fatal to the British officers and soldiers who expose themselves to view, even at more than double the distance of common musket shot."

The siege of Boston ended in March, 1776, when the British were forced to sail away to Canada and leave the Patriot troops in possession.

18 « LAST OF THE LORDS PROPRIETOR

It seems very sad that the Proprietorship of Maryland which had begun under the leadership of high-minded, shrewd and capable gentlemen like George, Cecil and the first Charles Calvert should end with a selfish weakling. Frederick Calvert, the sixth and last Lord Baltimore, bequeathed his great and flourishing Province to Henry Harford, an illegitimate son. Poor Henry was only fourteen years old when Governor Robert Eden, appointed by Henry's guardians, was forced to turn the government of Maryland over to a Committee of Safety.

When the time came for Governor Eden to flee aboard a British man-of-war, there was no violence. The rule of the Lords Proprietor came to an end as peacefully as it had begun, 144 years earlier.

As relations with the mother country steadily grew worse, the people of Maryland separated into two main groups. One consisted of Royalists or Tories who supported the Crown, the other, and very much more numerous, of Patriots or Whigs whom the British called Rebels.

Most of the Tidewater Big Wigs sided with the Crown. This was only natural since their fortunes depended upon the tobacco trade. When colonial governments forbade any traffic with the mother country, these planters faced ruin. However, quite a few powerful Big Wigs did support the cause of liberty with great energy and devotion.

A great majority of inhabitants of the northern and western parts of Maryland were fiercely patriotic and gave everything—often their lives and fortunes—to defend the cause of freedom.

Early in the War for Independence, Tidewater Maryland suffered a number of destructive raids. These attacks were made by Virginia Tories armed and inspired by Lord Dunmore, the Royal Governor of Virginia. Transported by ships of the Royal Navy, the Tories struck along the lower Eastern Shore. Ships, docks, tobacco barns and many homes were burned.

Lord Dunmore also tried to bribe local Indians into going on the warpath for him. Worse still, he offered Negro slaves held on the plantations their freedom if they would revolt and murder their masters. Fortunately for Maryland, nothing came of either of these evil projects.

The Maryland Convention reassembled at Annapolis in December, 1775. Alarmed by Lord Dunmore's raids along Chesapeake Bay, the delegates ordered several small ships to be armed with cannon as a protection against further attack.

Also, they resolved to raise 1,444 "regular" troops and enlisted a lot of militia—unfortunately for much too short terms of service.

The Convention sent a message to the Continental Congress saying it was in favor of stopping all oaths of allegiance to the Crown.

As determined as ever to govern themselves, the lawmakers in Annapolis declared: "The people of the Province have the sole and exclusive right of regulating the internal Government and policing of this Province."

The high point of this very important Maryland Convention came when Charles Carroll, who was said to be the richest man in all the colonies, urged that Maryland send representatives to consult with those of the other twelve colonies about drafting a formal Declaration of Independence.

19 « INDEPENDENCE AND SELF-GOVERNMENT

Once the Siege of Boston had ended with the King's white-wigged redcoats being driven out of their stronghold, the inhabitants of the United Colonies felt a new confidence in themselves. The War for Independence then really got underway.

In December, 1775, committees appointed by the Maryland Convention began to run the former Province.

Without a single objection, the Maryland Convention enthusiastically adopted a resolution of very great importance.

We, therefore, inhabitants of the Province of Maryland, firmly persuaded that it is necesary and justifiable to repel *force* by *force,* do approve of . . . opposition by arms to . . . British troops employed to enforce . . . the late acts and statutes of the British parliament for raising a revenue in America . . . and for destroying . . . the lives, liberties, and properties of the subjects in the United Colonies.

Because Lord Dunmore's attacks, which were backed by British sea power and the King's troops directly threatened their property and lives, Marylanders prepared for an all-out war with a wholehearted determination and enthusiasm they hadn't felt during the French and Indian Wars.

The King's Ministers made several sincere efforts to win over their rebellious subjects but, largely because of slow communications, nothing came of them.

At this time a good many true patriots were against complete independence. They feared that the United Colonies were much too weak and disorganized among themselves to win a war against the powerful armed forces of King George III.

On June 28, 1776, Charles Carroll arose in the Maryland Convention and in a stirring speech proclaimed that:

We, The Delegates of Maryland . . . assembled, do declare that the King of Great Britain has violated his compact with this people, and they owe no allegiance to him.

We have therefore thought it just and necessary to empower our deputies . . . to join with a majority of the United Colonies in declaring them free and independent States.

It was then decided that Maryland should send delegates to join with representatives of the twelve other colonies in preparing a formal declaration of independence.

Charles Carroll of Carrollton spoke stirringly for independence.

Even before this happened, Richard Henry Lee of Virginia had risen before the Congress assembled in Philadelphia to offer an epic resolution that: "The United Colonies will, and of right, be free and independent States!"

As fast as they could gallop, express riders travelled dusty roads to spread the news. Tremendous enthusiasm gripped the rebellious colonies. Liberty poles were raised in many a country town. Such a pole would be a slender tree from which the bark and all branches had been removed. Girls and women would twist spiral garlands of flowers about it. They also decorated the pole with gay ribbons, bright streamers and flags of all sorts. On the top of a proper liberty pole was placed a bright red stocking cap with a red-white-and-blue cockade stitched to one side.

In other places a noble tree would be dedicated to the cause of freedom and ornamented like the liberty poles. Men, women and children would join hands and dance about it to "Yankee Doodle," a new tune which had been played at the siege of Boston. This was the most popular song of the day.

Men kissed their wives and sweethearts goodbye, dropped everything and hurried off to enlist. There were bonfires galore, tar barrels were burned and fiercely patriotic speeches made by the hundreds. In many places, men believed to be Tories were pulled out of bed to be tarred and feathered, ridden on a rail or otherwise roughly handled.

Many Tories became frightened. They sold their properties and businesses for whatever they would bring and sailed away to Canada. Many, however, took refuge in the Bahamas, Barbados, Jamaica and other smaller British islands in the Caribbean.

Tories made of sterner stuff began to band together and raise troops called "independent companies." Generally, Tory soldiers wore black three-cornered hats, green uniform

Some Tories were ridden out of town on a rail.

coats and white waistcoats. Being familiar with the country, they did much to help scarlet-jacketed British generals fight an American style of war. Tories grew very bitter toward patriotic former friends, neighbors and even members of their own families.

As the War for Independence dragged on, fighting between Tories and Patriots became merciless. Both sides committed dreadful atrocities.

In Philadelphia still stands an impressive old, red-brick building topped by a graceful white bell tower. Today it is called Independence Hall, but in 1776 it was known as the State House. For many years it had served as the Capitol building for the Colony of Pennsylvania. It was in this handsome, elm-shaded structure that the Continental Congress reassembled early in June, 1776.

Already it was very hot for that time of year. Delegates from all the colonies began to ride in, all dusty, sunburned and very thirsty. While there were some loud-talking hotheads among the representatives, most of them were grave, level-headed and well-educated. These men fully understood the terrible risks they were taking when they pledged their lives, their fortunes and their sacred honor to defend the cause of freedom.

The weather grew hotter and hotter until candles melted and red-faced delegates continuously had to mop their streaming faces and fan themselves whenever they could.

On June 11, 1776, a committee composed of Thomas Jefferson, Benjamin Franklin, John Adams, Robert Livingstone and Roger Sherman was appointed to draft a Declaration of Independence. Jefferson wrote the Declaration almost entirely by himself. John Adams and Benjamin Franklin made a few changes in the wording of it.

Thanks to Lord Dunmore's raids, the Maryland delegates to Congress were well aware of what could happen to them, their families and their possessions if the United Colonies lost their fight for freedom.

On July 2, copies of the Declaration were circulated among the representatives. They approved it without dissent on July 4.

On August 2, 1776, the weather was hotter than ever. Their best clothes dark with sweat, and with trickles of perspiration running from under their wigs, the delegates assembled to sign a document which was to change the course of history—not only for America but for the entire world. One after another, representatives approached a wide desk and there, under the clear gray eyes of Thomas Jefferson, chairman of the drafting committee, they bent over to write their names.

Among those signing for Maryland was Charles Carroll—"of Carrollton," he added so that there could be no mistaking exactly who he was. Almost as rich as Charles Carroll was a lawyer named William Paca. He had led the fight in Maryland against the Stamp Act. Samuel Chase was no Big Wig but a lawyer, the son of a Baltimore parson. Chase was a huge man and had such broad, red-brown features that (behind his back of course) he was called "Bacon Face." Samuel Chase was a prominent leader of the Sons of Liberty. Tory-minded neighbors described him as "a ringleader of mobs, a foul-mouthed and inflaming son of discord." Finally there was Thomas Stone, also a shrewd and able lawyer.

The scratching of the delegates' goose quill pens across that famous sheet of parchment was soft, but the results of their writing echoed louder than thunderclaps in the halls of history.

After nearly one hundred and forty-four years the quest for true freedom begun by the brave men and women who landed at St. Mary's City in 1636 was about to end in victory. The spirits of all those Marylanders who had dared, sacrificed and suffered and who had often given their lives in search of liberty must have rejoiced when the last signatures were placed on one of the noblest documents ever conceived by human beings.

Samuel Chase, William Paca, Thomas Stone, and Charles Carroll signed the Declaration of Independence under John Hancock's bold signature.

Not always swiftly, news of the signing of the Declaration of Independence spread the length and breadth of the newly independent State of Maryland. Sometimes the tidings were brought to lonely frontier blockhouses and rough hamlets by runners who had followed winding and twisted trails. They had to keep their senses alert with every stride.

In the lowlands, men and boys mounted on ungainly, heavy-footed plow horses galumphed from one village to the next to tell what had happened in Independence Hall on the 4th of July, 1776.

On the broad grain fields aroud Frederick, Hagerstown and Westminster, tanned, bearded farmers stopped harvesting and, pushing broad-brimmed hats onto the backs of their heads, listened to winded riders give them the glorious news that they now were citizens of a free and independent State!

Among the age-rounded and blue-green mountains of western Maryland—which bore such odd names as Backbone, Big Savage, Negro and Meadow—many a lanky frontiersman would pick up his long rifle, sling on his tomahawk and a war bag containing his bullet mold and food for a few days. Finally he would pick up a pack of furs which would pay for powder and bullets. With the moth-eaten tail of a 'coon or foxskin cap slatting against his shoulders, he would turn to wave goodbye to his sorrowing family. Then he would follow a trail or descend a creek until it joined a rough track that eventually would take him to the closest trading post.

Other restless-eyed riflemen wearing hunting shirts and well-worn moccasins came in to the rally point. They showed up alone, or by twos and threes if they came from the same family—as was often the case.

Local Indians squatted in the background and looked on,

wooden-faced. They didn't show it, but they were worried
that so many armed white men should be getting together.
Were these tough pioneers about to go on the warpath?
They were, but for once not against Indians.

The factor of a trading post sat behind a greasy plank
table on which most likely stood· the scales he used for
weighing furs and trade goods. When he wasn't doing business or squirting tobacco juice onto the earthen floor, the
factor would swear in volunteers. It was a mighty solemn
moment when the frontiersman signed or, more often, made
his mark with a figure X on the enlistment rolls.

Once every Patriot in the countryside had been accounted
for, little groups of volunteers would sling packs, shoulder
rifles and set off with a long, loose-jointed stride for the
nearest mustering point. Cumberland Town was the largest
and farthest west of these gathering places.

Farther east on the farm lands surrounding Frederick,
Hagerstown and Westminster, where there were more
people living, many men and youths came in to volunteer.
By the dozen, big, blond and generally blue-eyed "Dutch-
men" (Germans) enrolled.

Quite often their wives and large broods of tow-headed
children riding in heavy-wheeled farm carts came along to
the enlisting place. Round-eyed, they stared at the unfamiliar
bustle and crowds of people. Dogs barked and children ran
about excitedly. Everybody discussed what independence
was going to mean for them. They also argued over what
should be done right away.

When the moment came for the volunteers to move out
there were painful partings, but seldom were they tearful
in the presence of men going off to a war from which many
were not likely to return. This did not mean, of course, that
there would not be plenty of weeping after the ragged little
file had set off under the blazing sun amid a shifting haze
of dust.

Small boys carrying wooden guns and looking mighty

serious would tramp after their elders till they got tired and turned back.

Not all volunteers from the iron mills north and west of Baltimore were accepted. Brawny, blackened iron workers were told to stay put and keep their furnace fires hot. Badly needed cannons, rifle barrels and all kinds of military hardware had to be forged for the Patriot armies that were gathering. In fact, all through the War for Independence the iron mills of Maryland supplied a very large proportion of weapons used by the American forces.

In north central Maryland, the recruiting office was usually in the town's most important tavern. Before the enlistment center rose a recently planted liberty pole.

In Annapolis, celebration of the great news was more glittering and impressive. Cannon thundered, cavalry units pranced down the major streets and foot troops grinned self-consciously as they paraded to the *rat-a-tat-tat* of drums and the shrilling of fifes.

Gentlemen, young and old, hurriedly got together what equipment they figured they'd need. Fashionable tailors stitched day and night turning out elegant uniforms for socially select units. Since most officers designed their own uniforms, very few of them looked much alike. Later on, though, uniforms were cut to officially approved styles and patterns.

All these exciting goings-on were watched from behind drawn blinds by deeply worried Tory Big Wigs. Most of them were wise enough to keep their true feelings to themselves. They dutifully appeared on the door stoops to wave at the passing detachments marching in the service of the newborn state. In private, they prayed for King George III and the success of his redcoated troops.

Along the Eastern Shore and in the Tidewater country around the lower part of southern Maryland, the news was spread by barefooted countrymen wearing ragged homespuns and fraying straw hats. They paddled dugout canoes or sailed up the creeks and rivers in swift little sloops.

When the Tidewater people heard about the great happenings in Philadelphia, there wasn't quite the same rejoicing that prevailed farther north. Nevertheless, many fishermen quietly quit mending nets, and oystermen stopped repairing boats they wouldn't use until cold weather set in.

Quite a few Oronookos whose tobacco-growing lands were wearing out were glad of an excuse to quit farming and start over as soldiers.

On public and private docks gathered groups of well-dressed planters and their sons. Maybe an overseer or two would be among the volunteers. They mingled freely with down-at-the-heel former tenants, small merchants, trappers and gaunt, wild-looking men from the upper rivers. When these last spoke they often used quaint old English phrases which hadn't been heard for years along the Tidewater.

Sooner or later a sizeable vessel would sail into sight and tie up to take on board the waiting volunteers. As she raised sail a few cheers were heard. Later, the soft sobbing of womenfolk and children floated out over the warm, smooth water.

Thus Maryland gathered her Patriot sons from far and near. With heartfelt prayers she sent them forth to suffer and fight and, if necessary, to give their lives. They were determined that those ideals which, so long ago, had brought Lord Baltimore's first settlers to St. Mary's City should not perish from the earth.

BIBLIOGRAPHY

ANDREWS, MATTHEW PAGE, *History of Maryland*. New York: Double-day, 1929.

FOOTNER, HULBERT, *Rivers of the Eastern Shore*. New York: Farrar & Rinehart, 1944.

GABRIEL, WOOD, *The Winning of Freedom* (Pageant of America Series). New Haven: Yale University Press, 1923.

HALL, CLAYTON COLMAN (ed.), *Early Narratives of Maryland*. New York: Charles Scribner's Sons, 1910.

————, *The Lords Baltimore and the Maryland Palatinate*. Baltimore: Nunn and Company, 1904.

MORRIS, RICHARD B., *Encyclopedia of American History*. New York: Harper & Bros., 1953.

SEMMES, RAPHAEL, *Captains and Mariners of Early Maryland*. Baltimore: Johns Hopkins Press, 1937.

STEVENS, OLIVER, *Annapolis*. New York: Dodd, Mead, 1937.

TUNIS, EDWIN, *Colonial Living*. New York: World Publishing Co., 1957.

WILSTACH, PAUL, *Tidewater Maryland*. New York: Bobbs, Merrill, 1931.

The February, 1964, and August, 1967, issues of *American Heritage* also contain material of interest on the Maryland Colony.

IMPORTANT DATES

1608—Captain John Smith explores Chesapeake Bay.

1632—George Calvert, First Lord Baltimore granted Charter by Charles I. He dies before it is sealed.

1633—*Ark* and *Dove* arrive at St. Mary's.

1638—February. Kent Island captured from William Claiborne.

1644—Claiborne returns and defeats Marylanders at Spa Creek.

1649—King Charles I beheaded. Commonwealth established. Act of Tolerance passed.

1650—The Dutch establish Fort Casimir on Eastern Shore.

1653—Cromwell becomes Lord Protector.

1658—Maryland restored to Lord Proprietor, Cecil Calvert, by Cromwell.

1660—Commonwealth ends. Charles II becomes King of England.

1664—British capture New York and end Dutch rule.

1675—Charles Calvert succeeds to Proprietorship.

1685—Charles II dies. James II succeeds. Deposed in 1688. William III succeeds.

1689–1697—King William's War (First French & Indian War).

1691—Sir Lionel Copley, First Royal Governor appointed.

1702–1713—Queen Anne's War (Second French & Indian War).

1715—Rule restored to the Lord Proprietor of Maryland by George I.

1729—Baltimore Town chartered.

1750—Heirs of William Penn win Maryland territory.

1751—Frederick, Sixth Lord Baltimore succeeds.

1754—Seven Years War (Third French & Indian War).

1755—Defeat of Braddock.
1763—Chief Pontiac's Conspiracy.

1763–1767—Mason and Dixon survey border between Maryland and Pennsylvania.

1771—Frederick Calvert dies.

1773—Boston Tea Party.

1774—*Peggy Stewart* burned.

—September-October. First Continental Congress meets.

1775—April. Battle of Lexington and Concord.

—May. Second Continental Congress meets.

—June. Battle of Bunker Hill.

—June. George Washington named Chief of the Continental Forces.

1776—March. British evacuate Boston.

—July 4. Declaration of Independence adopted.

PLACES TO VISIT

Below is a list of several historical sites in Maryland which readers may wish to see for themselves.

ANNAPOLIS

LIBERTY TREE. It was under this giant tulip poplar that the early colonists signed a peace treaty with the Susquehannock Indians in 1652. The tree is believed to be six hundred years old.

WILLIAM PACA HOUSE. Built in 1763, this was the home of a signer of the Declaration of Independence. Walking tours, conducted by Historic Annapolis, Inc., leave from the Paca House. Daily, JulyAugust, 1:30 P.M. $1. Other historical sites tours may be arranged.

STATE HOUSE. This oldest state house still in use in the United States was built in 1772. Among other displays is the oldest official American flag used in the American Revolution. Daily, except Christmas Day, 9 A.M.–5 P.M. Free.

OLD TREASURY. This is the oldest (1735) public building in Maryland.

BALTIMORE

MARYLAND HISTORICAL SOCIETY. Museum and library of the state's history. June 15–September 14, Monday-Friday, 9 A.M–4 P.M. September 15–June 14, Monday-Friday, to 5 P.M. Saturday, except August and most holidays, 9 A.M.–1 P.M. Free.

CARROLL MANSION. This was the last home of Charles Carroll "of Carrollton." He died here in 1832, the last surviving signer of the Declaration of Independence. Tuesday-Friday, 10:30 A.M.–4:30 P.M. Sunday, 1:00–5:00 P.M. Closed January 1, May 30, Labor Day, and Christmas Day. Free.

MOUNT CLARE STATION. An earlier home of Charles Carroll, this oldest house in Baltimore was built in 1754. April-October, Tuesday-Saturday, 11 A.M.–3:45 P.M. (November-March, to 3:15 P.M.). Sunday from 2:00 P.M. Closed January 1, Thanksgiving, December 24, 25, and 31. Guided tours, 75¢; children under 12 with adults, 25¢.

PEALE MUSEUM. This is the oldest museum building in America and is devoted to Baltimore's history. Tuesday-Saturday, 10:30 A.M.–4:30 P.M. Sunday, 1:30 P.M.–5:30 P.M. Closed most holidays, Sundays from May 30–Labor Day, and Saturdays in August. Free.

CAMBRIDGE

OLD TRINITY CHURCH. Dating to about 1675, this is believed to be the oldest church in the United States still in use. Daily except Tuesday, 9 A.M.–5 P.M. Free.

EASTON

WYE OAK STATE PARK. Here can be seen the official State Tree of Maryland, a giant white oak said to be four hundred years old. Nearby is a restored one-room schoolhouse of the eighteenth century.

CHESAPEAKE BAY MARITIME MUSEUM. This museum is devoted to the history of Chesapeake Bay. Tuesday-Sunday, 10 A.M.–4 P.M. Closed January 1, December 25. Adults 50¢, children 25¢.

THIRD HAVEN MEETING HOUSE. William Penn worshiped in this old (1682–84) church on the site of the original Quaker settlement. Free.

ST. MARY'S CITY

BENCH ON ST. MARY'S RIVER. On this spot, Leonard Calvert's ships, the *Ark* and the *Dove,* first touched the mainland of Maryland.

LEONARD CALVERT MONUMENT. On this spot, Maryland's first government was established.

FREEDOM OF CONSCIENCE STATUE. This statue by Hans Schuler stands as a symbol of freedom of religion in the Maryland Colony.

"OLD" STATE HOUSE. This replica of the first Capitol of Maryland is located near the site of the original structure that was built in 1676. May-September, Daily, 10 A.M–5 P.M. (rest of year, to 4:00 P.M.). Closed some holidays. Free.

SALISBURY

MASON-DIXON LINE MARKER. The coats of arms of Lord Baltimore and William Penn may be seen on this relic of the famous survey of the Maryland-Pennsylvania boundary.

UPPER MARLBORO

Although the Maryland tobacco industry went into decline after the American Revolution, this town has remained a tobacco center for three hundred years and still cultivates the plant in much the same manner as its colonial ancestors. Visitors may wish to attend tobacco auctions in the area, mid-April to mid-July.

Times and admission prices are subject to change without notice.

INDEX